A New Understanding of Life

Ralph A. Steadman

A New Understanding of Life
2010, first print edition

© Copyright Ralph A. Steadman 2010.

The author asserts the moral right to be named
as author of the work

Front cover photography courtesy HubbleSite, NASA,
and the Space Telescope Science Institute

ISBN 978-1-4461-0135-3

Contents

	Page
Foreword	4
Introduction	5
1. Landmarks on the Inner Journey	7
2. The Channelling Process	12
3. Modern Science and Ancient Wisdom	15
4. Energy and Intelligence	24
5. Visitors from Space	33
6. Planetary Influences and Astrology	40
7. Kali Yuga and the rise of "Numan"	48
8. Energy Fields and the Chakra System	55
9. Thought and Karma	65
10. Thought and Health	74
11. Children	84
12. Karmic Reward	87
13. Prayer, Health and Healing	96
14. Planetary Change and Human Survival	107
15. The Life of the Universe	116
16. Dimensions and Dimensional Travel	124
17. Affirmations and 1st Dimensional entities	134
18. "The Fall", Guides and Angels	143
19. Sound and Music	152
20. Individual and Mass Ascension	162
21. Summation	178
Further Reading	179
Acknowledgements	180
Index	181
About the Author	182

Foreword

So many things about the human condition remain hidden and mysterious that it is difficult to reach any conclusions to guide us in these times of rapid and confusing change.

It is here that Ralph Steadman's clear, detailed and consistent channelling can reveal many of the answers, so that we can see human beings for the complex and subtle creatures that they really are.

This book takes us step by step through the stages of our creation, spiritual evolution, awakening and liberation. This channelling provides a completely new understanding that is clear, profound and well adapted to the special needs of the vital time in which we live.

Stewart Wilson
Author

Introduction

There is at present a heightened stream of consciousness coming across the universe, which is impacting the Earth with increasing intensity, and is affecting people in many different ways. All are sensing that something is about to happen, and are reacting to the situation according to their own characters.

At the one end of the spectrum, there is an increase in lawlessness, and a desire to break out of all the restraints of conventional behaviour and morality. At the other, there is an increasing recognition that Humanity has depleted the resources of the planet to such an extent that the survival of many of the life-forms, and even the survival of the human race itself, is gravely endangered. Somewhere in the middle are the people who are religious. Those who are already committed to one or other religion are becoming more and more convinced that their way is correct, so that there is a rise of fundamentalism in many faiths, and those who are already fundamentalist are becoming increasingly militant.

On the fringes of religion there are those of a *New Age* tendency, who claim to be spiritual and who are becoming more attracted to the idea of *2012* when, according to ancient Mayan prophecies, the end of the present world cycle will come about - and widely different ideas of what *that* means to Humanity are being hotly debated!

Science and scientists are not to be left out, and the changing cosmic influence means that as new discoveries are being made, some of the "holy cows" which have formed the basis of scientific knowledge for centuries are now being questioned, causing hot dispute in many specialisms, while the more fundamentalist scientists are attacking the basic philosophy behind religion – and religions themselves – with increasing virulence. However, a small but growing minority of scientists, as they make new discoveries, are starting to speak in a language which is not too far removed from that used by mystics throughout the ages. Some are even starting to bridge the gap between Science and Religion in their own personal beliefs!

Meanwhile the majority of people are totally confused by the growing number of different views regarding the most ancient question – What is Life about? Although their curiosity has been stirred by the new energies – and many are now having various kinds of psychic experiences, heightened intuition and inexplicable healings – they wonder if there is any truth in religious philosophy, and if so which brand of religion has the most truth in it. Or are those scientists correct who maintain that life is merely the result of chance events which happened some billions of years ago, and who say that human beings survive only in the genes which they pass on to their descendents?

It is to these people – the silent majority – that this book is addressed, and hopefully will provide a starting point for their own inner quest. I emphasise that it is meant only as a starting point, as I am well aware that we are all individuals and must make up our own minds about what we believe. For far too long people have been told *what* to believe, and have allowed themselves to be led meekly into the mindset which the hierarchy – political or religious – has decided that they should have. And even today, in our "enlightened" times, there are countless millions who are afraid to think for themselves, and say what they think, for fear of running foul of religious, political or social leaders!

But whichever category of reader you are – Scientist, Theologian or one of the silent majority – there is a *reason* for you to be reading this book at the moment. Nothing happens by chance and very often, looking back on our life, we see that something which appeared at the time to be a simple coincidence proved with hindsight to be the start of a new chapter of experience or understanding. Possibly, for some of you, reading this book may have the same effect. Whether or not that is the case, I hope that you get as much enjoyment out of reading the book as I have had in writing it.

Ralph A. Steadman
November 2010

1. Landmarks on the Inner Journey

Spiritual progression can't be mapped as a straight-line graph – life just isn't like that at all. We may go along for many years with nothing apparently happening on the spiritual front, and then suddenly be faced with a life-changing event which sets us off in a completely different direction. After such an event there is often a period of time when nothing remarkable happens, followed by another momentous happening. So if we plot our "spiritual graph" it may often look like a series of sharp inclines followed by horizontal plateaux. And to give you some idea of how this book came to be written I would like to map out some of the most important spiritual mileposts on my journey.

My introduction to the paranormal began when I was 21, and my spiritual mentor was Aunty Margaret, one of my beloved late wife's many aunts. Many years before, she had been a top-rank medium serving the Marylebone Circuit of Spiritualist Churches in London – then the most prestigious circuit in the world. I was in the Army at the time, at a camp some 40 miles from home. Recently married, I was looking for a local flat or house to rent, so that my new wife, Eleanor, could come and join me.

We were staying with my in-laws then, and I travelled home from the camp every Saturday, getting the same bus, train and local bus every week, and always arriving at about the same time. One week I got a lift which cut my initial bus journey in half, but left me with half an hour to spare in a small village on the bus route, while the bus that I would have caught at the camp gates trundled round the countryside. I went into the local pub and asked if there were any flats for rent in the area, and the landlord sent me to a house just over the road.

I spoke to the owner, and we arranged for me to rent a flat in the house (subject, of course to my wife's approval.) Then I had to rush across to the bus stop, just in time to catch the bus. The rest of the journey passed as usual and I arrived home at the normal time.

When I got there, Aunty Margaret was giving "readings" to all the family, and without saying a word I stood by the door and cynically watched all these gullible people being told what I considered to be a lot of rubbish. At the end, I was invited to sit at the table for a reading, but refused to have anything to do with this charade, until my new wife, in no uncertain terms said, "Sit down!"

Aunty Margaret's first words shook me: "You are going to live in that house that you have just been to see. Eleanor will teach at the local school and will be interviewed for the job by three men. You will be very happy there but will leave after having spent *exactly* one year in the house." Then she went on to give many other detailed predictions.

Of course, everyone wanted to know what all that had been about, so I told them – and everything that she predicted came true, even down to the fact that we had to move out of the house a year to the day from when we moved in. Although I wondered about the accuracy of these predictions, I eventually just put it down to coincidence.

Many years later Aunty Margaret took me one evening to a local community centre, where she ran Spiritualist services. I sat at the back of the hall, well away from the platform at the front, so that I could see everything which happened without being personally involved. At least that was what I thought! At the start of the clairvoyance the Spiritualist minister conducting the service pointed in my direction and said, "I want to come to that young man at the back." I sank down in my chair and pretended not to be there. However, he persisted, and eventually the people sitting in front of me turned round and hissed, "He is talking to *you*" – so I *had* to take notice. I still remember his first words: "You have a great work to do for Spiritualism." He carried on and said a lot more, most of which I couldn't understand, and when I asked Aunty Margaret afterwards why he was talking about a lot of dead people, it freaked me out when she said that they had been there wanting to communicate with me.

So I said, "That is all a load of rubbish – and I will prove it." Over the next five years I attended as many Spiritualist church services and demonstrations as I could – but eventually I ended up by proving to my own satisfaction that it was all genuine.

The next breakthrough happened many years later when I was working away from home in a city which I didn't really know. One evening, with nothing to do, I went to the local Spiritualist Church. After the service I spoke to the president and asked her if they ever had anyone speaking about Reincarnation, and she said "You should have been here last week. Mr X was the medium, and he is an expert on it." So I asked for his phone number, phoned him up and went to see him. Although I was a complete stranger he didn't seem at all surprised to see me. He spoke to me for about a couple of hours and what he told me sent my spiritual development off in a totally different direction. I never saw him again but I remain eternally grateful to him.

I then stayed on a spiritual plateau for almost twenty years, before going to a small Spiritualist Church and hearing an address on Cosmic Influences by a famous local medium. After the service, I said to my daughter, "Well, what did you think of that?" "I didn't understand a word of it," was her reply. I said, "That is the most amazing address I have ever heard: I must go and see that man" – and see him I did. I was with him for only half an hour, during which he kept telling me things, and saying ....."but you already know that," – and I realised that I *did* already know it. He was just reminding me of things which I knew *but didn't know that I knew.*

The next change which came into my life was not only a spiritual change but a massive life change – my beloved Eleanor died. After 38 years of marriage, the last seven of which had been as close to perfection as one can get in a relationship, she succumbed to a slow and painful form of cancer. However, after two years she contacted my youngest daughter through a medium and said, "Tell your father that it is time he stopped grieving. There is no need for it. I am going to bring a new lady to him in the near future who will be with him for the rest of his life – and he will know that she is the right one before next Spring."

Although I am not by nature a swearing man, my reply to that was "Not – – likely!" But following a chain of coincidences I met Sybil just six weeks later – and the rest, as they say, is history. And although it does seem as if I am being disloyal to Eleanor in saying it I have to admit that my spiritual development over the last 17 years has been far more rapid than in the whole of my previous life.

I didn't think that there would be any more major revelations in my life after I retired, but then one of my daughters emigrated to Western Australia, followed by her two sisters and one of her brothers. I went to see them several times, usually with Sybil but on one memorable occasion without her. She was looking after her aged mother, who was very frail and not expected to live much longer, so I made that trip alone.

While I was in Australia I had some memorable spiritual experiences, including being initiated as a member of one of the local aboriginal tribes and then later experiencing a higher-grade initiation. Each initiation was done in an ancient ritual called "foot-ochre-ing." "Ochre" is a kind of earth, and there are several colours (each presumably denoting a different mineral content) of which I know only red, yellow and black. The ritual is very long and complicated – to the best of my recollection each time it lasted about two hours, although at the time it didn't seem anywhere near that long.

The ritual starts when the prospective initiate takes off his/ her shoes and socks, and has the feet massaged with kangaroo oil. Then, when this has started to sink into the skin, the ochre is applied. It is a powdery substance, and is massaged well into the feet, ankles and shins. The prospective initiate is then asked questions, such as, "What do you see? What do you feel? Where are you? Who is with you?" I don't know what properties the ochre has, whether it is soporific or hallucinogenic, but after a while the subject becomes drowsy and starts to see visions.

I have never been clairvoyant, and up to this time had only a general ability to *sense* non-physical vibrations, but as my first session progressed I found that I was able to answer the questions more easily, and was actually *seeing* things happening. On one occasion I was asked to describe where I was, and I saw a campfire in the bush, with all my family standing round. I was able to describe each of them, and was particularly taken by the tribal matriarch – the Grandmother – who was in the middle of the group. She was very short, but extremely well-built – I think that her girth would have been literally more than her height. She had the most wonderful smile on her face, and radiated pure Love to all the members of the tribe (who were, of course, all her relatives.)

I am not aware of the hierarchy of initiations, but in my case I had the red foot-ochre first, and the yellow foot-ochre several months later. On the first occasion I had been initiated by a white woman, who had spent so much time working with the aboriginals that she had been given the honour of being allowed to initiate non-aboriginals into the tribe. However, on the second occasion I was introduced to a woman who was one of the most senior of all tribal elders. I am not allowed to mention her name, so I will call her P.

When I entered P's house, she was busy talking to another person, so she told me to go through to the verandah, where I found the seeress of the local tribe. I looked at her in amazement, knowing that I knew her – but I couldn't remember from where. I said, "I know you" – and then remembered. "You were the grandmother!" And indeed, she was the same woman that I had seen in my vision. She smiled and nodded. That was the start of a memorable afternoon.

During the initiation ceremony there were several people from different nationalities present. The format of the ritual was the same, but this time the questions were more searching, and my answers more precise and detailed. I saw myself in three different lives as an aboriginal, gave my names and those of my tribes and described the places where the tribes lived, some of which were verified by those present. I recognised two of those present as relatives in past lives, and one particularly poignant moment was when I described in detail the coming-of-age ritual of one of them – then my son. The pride which I felt caused me to sob uncontrollably – something which is totally out of character with my rather detached Aquarian personality.

After the emotional roller-coaster of my initiation, I was talking with P, and she asked – with a mischievous twinkle in her eyes – when we had met in a previous life. I was immediately taken back to Atlantis, where I was some sort of local dignitary, and I saw a little girl playing. I knew that she was my granddaughter, and was the only person who could "wind me round her little finger". I described the scene to P and she said "Yes, you were my *damu*."

She used the aboriginal word which literally means "grandfather", and from that time on she introduced me to others as "my *damu*." But that had an amazing result: in aboriginal society the words signifying older relatives have a double meaning, because they also mean "spiritual counsellor". So that when I was introduced as P's *damu* – and she herself was so revered by everyone – I was regarded almost in awe, which was a very uncomfortable feeling.

On one occasion in Australia I was introduced to the daughter of the seeress – a lady who was also a seeress. As soon as I met her she said, "You are a wizard." I was a little taken aback, but then she explained that, in aboriginal lore, a particular bone-formation on the forehead is the mark of a wizard, one who has special powers – and I have that very formation on *my* forehead.

I said at the beginning that certain events kick-start us into a new phase of spiritual progression, and my time in Australia certainly did that for me: when I came back my clairsentience took off at a rapid rate. This became the trigger for me to channel this book, and it has also helped me to remember some of my past lives.

I have now had flashbacks to about fifteen previous lives, in places like Atlantis, ancient Egypt and Medieval and Revolutionary France. And from time to time, when meeting new people, I can "remember" what we were to each other in a past life.

I don't know if my Australian adventure was the last of my spiritual breakthroughs and have no idea of what the future holds for me. However, one thing is certain – it will certainly be interesting!

2. The Channelling Process

Although I am not clairvoyant, I have a certain degree of sensitivity, and so am able to pick up information about people or situations, which over the years has developed into an ability to "channel". Channelling is a form of mediumship in which the person involved – known as "the instrument" – allows him/ herself to be used as a mouthpiece for a discarnate being, usually someone who *was* a human being but has now passed into a higher dimension. There are different levels of channelling: in some cases the medium goes into trance and has no idea at all of what is being said, waking up only after the channelling has finished. In my case, when I channel it feels as though I am standing behind myself listening to what is being said: I am fully conscious, and aware of what is happening, yet have no control whatsoever over the content of the message.

Towards the end of 2007, I was told by several mediums that I had to write a channelled book, as there were several discarnate beings who were waiting for me to make myself ready for them to work through me. I was to sit at a computer and write down whatever I was inspired to say. I must admit that at the time I was not particularly happy at the thought: I had no problems with the writing side – I am reasonably computer-literate and am able to type fairly quickly – but the thought of having to undertake a major project in my retirement, instead of just putting my feet up and enjoying life, was quite daunting.

But I was told that the information which I would be able to transmit would be for the eventual benefit of Humanity, and would help to start to heal the rift between Science and Religion which has existed for the last few hundred years. Now this was something which aroused my curiosity: although I had for a long time been interested in religious philosophy, I had absolutely no knowledge whatsoever about scientific matters.

And so it was when, early in 2007, I sat at the computer for the first time – with some misgiving – that I said, "OK then, if you want to channel something through me then let's get going." And to my amazement I started to get some information through, which I duly typed.

I found the first session reasonably interesting, although it did not add greatly to my own philosophy, and so a few days later I sat once more and received a second instalment. This started a series of sittings – 110 in all – which eventually lasted over a period of slightly more than two years. Each one was usually about an hour long, although when I was interrupted some were much shorter. The individual sessions produced anything from a few lines up to several pages, depending on the circumstances. The rate of production of the material was not very consistent: on some occasions, I sat down and everything flowed very smoothly, on others I sat down out of a sense of duty and received virtually nothing. At some periods I spent time almost every day in channelling, at others several months went by without me having the slightest interest in writing at all.

One thing which interested me while I was channelling is that the individual discarnate beings – with one exception – did not identify themselves. I was told that the work should be judged on its own merits, rather than relying on some famous name in order to promote it – and I agree completely. I was told that they would come from many different backgrounds, and I believe that some of the early ones to come through were Classical philosophers. At least, that is what I was told by some of my mediumistic friends, who could see them.

But others were from other different cultural traditions, among which were Australian Aboriginal, North American Indian, African, Chinese and Maori/Polynesian. In fact, the last one was the only being who identified himself by name: he was Tutanekai – a legendary Polynesian hero. In most cases I could not understand why I should have attracted someone of that culture, with the possible exception of Australian Aboriginal, as I have Australian friends who are aboriginal.

But the lack of ability to identify the individuals by name did have some drawbacks for a time. I believe that there were about fifteen individuals who channelled through me, and sometimes I would channel some information which – when I later read it through – I realised was basically the same in concept as something else which I had already channelled, but expressed in different words. At first I was inclined to just delete the whole passage, but then I realised that the anomaly was caused by the fact that, although the content was the same, the second passage had been dictated by a different being, who had naturally used his own words and particular style to emphasise the message. Most of the information given by different beings was totally harmonious with that given by others, and when it appeared contradictory it was more a difference of emphasis rather than one of substance.

Sometimes it was obvious that a different being was speaking, from the way in which he started. I say "he", as I am not aware that there were any feminine beings who influenced me, although it is quite possible that there were. It was just that none of the energies *felt* feminine at the time when I channelled them. But usually one passage merged seamlessly with its predecessor, without any obvious change of source – and this was made easier by the fact that in most cases the beings used the plural *we*, rather than the singular *I*. I did not ask specifically about this aspect of the channelling at the time, although I did get the impression that, at the level of advancement where all of them existed, the *self* was of less importance than *the whole*: it was almost as though I was being contacted by a committee, speaking through a spokesman, who later stepped back and gave way to a different one. But this was not completely consistent, and there were several occasions when *I* and *we* were used interchangeably.

So what of the content? Although much of what was channelled was new to me, and particularly the passages about the different dimensions and the entities which inhabit them, I could see some connections with the doctrines of Christianity. I have little knowledge of the detailed teachings of other religions, but it is possible that devotees of those religions might also find connections. But it was obvious that the beings who came through to give information were trying very hard to avoid aligning the philosophy too closely to any one religion: for instance, they went to great lengths to avoid giving a name to the prime Creative Force, suggesting only that the reader should insert his/ her preferred name in the appropriate places.

But if that side of the information was sometimes obscure to me, the scientific side was completely unknown. Although as a linguist I am familiar with scientific words such as "cosmologist" and "quantum physics", anything beyond a dictionary definition is totally beyond me, and I found it fascinating to be given information which *appeared* to be scientific explained in a very simple way. Whether or not it can stand up to the rigorous scrutiny of real scientists is not for me to judge.

In editing the material, I had the choice of gathering together all items under the different topics covered or leaving the text completely in the date order of the channelling. I tried the former, but found that because of the different styles of expression of individuals, and the continual referring back to what had gone before, the resultant text was difficult to read, so I have reproduced the original as it was given, with only grammatical editing. I have substituted asterisks for the dates of individual channellings, to show how the material was received.

Finally, I realise that there are many people who consider the word "negative" to be judgemental, when used to describe actions or conditions, and prefer to use words like "inappropriate", "unsuitable" or "challenging". I have no dispute with that mindset, but for reasons of uniformity I have left the original text as it was given, and would ask readers to substitute their own preferred words where they think it more appropriate.

3. Modern Science and Ancient Wisdom

Since the beginning of time there has been an invisible structure round Earth – what you might call a framework, or a network of points which form a mesh capable of receiving the intelligence and the life which streams across the universe to feed your planet. This network receives, sifts and filters information so that what is received on the surface – and particularly by all the denizens of your world – is in a form which may be readily and easily accepted and assimilated for the continuation and the furtherance of the life-forms. It allows the growth and evolution of each species in a way which you might call exponential – continual growth and multiplication of forms. This leads to an outburst of energy, which can only be dreamt of in human terms, for it is beyond the imagination of most mortals. Yet on our plane we can see what is happening, and can only marvel at – and praise – the Creative Force which brought it into being in the first place.

With limited human vision, Humanity is currently of the opinion that the number of life-forms and species on the planet is diminishing, but this is not so. For as one physical species disappears, two more non-physical ones come into being, so that there is not a diminution of forms, but in fact an increase. The difference is that the new forms are on a wavelength which is not immediately perceptible to human consciousness, and so in ignorance it is thought that there is an overall decrease.

But as more and more human beings evolve to the level where they are able to interact with the next dimension, there will be a greater understanding of what Reality truly is – and that will open a new horizon for the next stage of human evolution. You have a phrase in your vocabulary which says that "the grass is greener on the other side of the hill:" in this case, it is literally true, as what is at present hidden from all but a few of you is vastly more interesting, radiant and truly *alive* than anything which you can currently imagine.

You are rapidly approaching the time when there will be a true recognition of the reality of Creation, and at the same time there will come a dawning of the concept that you are part of it – that you, in fact are co-creators, and that you may destroy or create, according to whatever your current mindset is.

There are those among you who believe that Humanity is destroying the Earth, and they believe that the Earth cannot survive much more of the deprivations and degradations which are being heaped upon her. But this is false, for the Earth is in fact a sentient being, and she will eventually react to protect herself, in a way which will not necessarily be for the immediate benefit of Humanity. But remember that the survival of the Earth and the survival of the human species are not synonymous: the Earth could survive – and would survive – even if there were no human beings on it, whereas human beings could survive on a completely different planet, if the Earth eventually became too inhospitable. But the original plan for the Earth was to create an environment in which a multitude of species – including your own – could live, grow and evolve in total harmony, and in this context Humanity is indeed hindering the possibility of a favourable outcome. So something needs to be done – and is already in the process of being done. For there are cosmic changes afoot which will bring human beings face to face with their own place in the universe.

At the moment the human experiment has gone almost as far as is possible, for you are faced daily with the inhumanity of humans to others: you have wars, racial, religious and political divisions, and there is more and more distrust between each of the nations of the Earth. Many of you bewail the demise of "the old days" – times when despite hardships there seemed to be much more friendship and camaraderie. You compare these times with the present, when hatred and suspicion seem to be rife everywhere. But you are not aware of some of the fundamental laws of the universe, and particularly that of action and reaction, Cause and Effect. You know that it is one of the laws of mundane Physics, of course, but you do not see it in a wider context. Everything in Creation tends towards balance, so that whatever happens to disturb that balance has in its very core – like the inner life potential of a seed – the energy of the opposite. You have the analogy of the pendulum: when it swings towards its one extremity, more and more forces are dragging it back to stop it going too far, and eventually the two opposing forces will become equal. Thereafter it needs only a small change to start the pendulum moving in the opposite direction.

This is the point which the human race is rapidly approaching. You are almost at the furthest point away from absolute equilibrium, so that inexorably the time is approaching when those forces dragging you back towards the ideal of perfection will overcome those which drive you away, and then – as you say – the tide will turn.

But here we come to another phenomenon: that of acceleration. For as a stone falls to earth, it accelerates, due to what you call the Force of Gravity. And so it will be in your human terms when you reach the moment of the return towards the perfection of equilibrium. For there will be what you call a *ground swell* of energy which will impel you, faster and faster, until you are hurtling back towards your true destiny at a rate which is at present unimaginable. And in that headlong race towards perfection, all the divisions which currently exist among you will gradually disappear – will simply dissolve away – until the whole of Humanity is moving together towards the glory of its ultimate destiny.

* * *

Once more we make contact with you. I say "we", for it is not just one being who will be contacting you and giving you the information: it is a group of beings, each of whom will have his own specific input. Each of us followed a similar pattern during our earthly life, always seeking to understand and to interpret the mysteries of life, how it was created, what was its purpose and how it was organised in practical terms. But from that same starting point each of us travelled a widely different path, for each had his own character and background, and each was aiming to understand a specific aspect of Creation.

But now we have a broader view of what is the overall reality, so that our differences during our earthly lives can be seen for what they really were – differences of aspect and not of substance. You already know that by looking at an object from several different angles you can gain a better appreciation of what it really is, whereas looking from one direction only – however keen the observation – can give at best only an impression of the object's true essence. What human beings tend to do is to view everything from a single perspective, and disregard – or even worse, dispute – the validity of the opinions of others who look from another direction.

This is why you have so many divisions in your earthly life, caused by the inability to accept that there are other ways of looking at things – and these divisions are particularly marked when you are considering matters which are intangible, such as ideal states of human behaviour, social organisation, political strategy and the like. Even a simple definition of one of the abstract virtues – truth, beauty, justice, or compassion can provoke dissension, so it is little wonder that when it comes to a discussion of the most important matter of all that you have an apparent chasm between the views of different factions.

And what is the most important matter in human life? It is the question of the very nature of Humanity itself. What are human beings, and what was the process by which they were created? How do they fit into the overall scheme of Creation itself? Is each individual merely a passing phenomenon, or is there a permanence beyond the ephemeral nature of the earthly life? All of these individual questions are part of the main question, which has been expressed by human beings through the ages who have asked "What am I?"

This same question is still fiercely debated in your intellectual circles, on many different levels: you have your scientists who try to reduce everything to a level of biological simplicity, and who maintain that the human species came into being purely as a result of an evolution of simpler forms of life. For them the initial impetus was merely an accident of different chemicals coming together. On the other hand, you have your religious people, who maintain that the creation of everything occurred in the space of a short time – in some versions as little as a week – and came about by the actions of a single Creator.

But who – or what – that Creator was causes even more furious divisions, and there are even heated arguments about his name. He is seen as a masculine Creator, of course, as the rulers of most earthly nations – and certainly of earthly religions – are all male.

In the sphere of religion, you have the rise of fundamentalism in which different religious sects become increasingly extreme, promoting literal word-for-word interpretation of the meanings of their diverse holy books. This fundamentalism does not of itself create more divisions – the divisions are there already – but what it does is emphasise those divisions. Instead of seeking to understand the common factors which exist in different religions, it usually concentrates on the more extreme beliefs – and so it exacerbates the hostility between the religions.

As a result of all these divisions, you have the current state of Humanity on your planet – a state of division and discord. You have more and more differences between political, religious and social factions, which lead to hostility and warfare, to deprivation and disease, to fear and suppression. The differences between individual factions are becoming more pronounced, and you now have the phenomenon of opposites: a small number of people on earth are immensely wealthy, while the vast majority are extremely poor. Large numbers of people are hungry – in fact many are starving – while one of the major diseases of the wealthy is obesity, with all its attendant problems. In the affluent sectors of your society you have increasing numbers of possessions, and yet you have more and more stressful lives.

Also, in the mad race towards material gain you are depleting the physical resources of the planet at an alarming rate, even to the level where many of your scientists are warning of global catastrophe, and some are even questioning the possibility of the survival of the human race itself. This has been brought into sharper focus by the happenings of the past few years, where the extremes of weather conditions have shown you how little you are able to control the powers of the elements, and the increasing frequency of unusual natural events is leading many to talk in terms of a Doomsday Scenario, in which Humanity comes to the end of physical existence.

Of course, this is where some religious extremists among you – the so-called "End-timers" – are in their element, as they can quote the prophecies of ancient times to show how the human species is now facing its Apocalypse. Naturally, to them the only way of salvation is by following a belief in their own particular religious system. But as the followers of that system make up less than a third of the current population of the world, it doesn't give much hope for the rest of the planet's inhabitants.

* * *

Throughout the ages, Humanity has asked the fundamental question – "What am I?" But the more the question has been asked, the more different answers have been given. That has only served to confuse, so that eventually most human beings have just given up even trying to understand the mysteries of life, preferring instead to study other, more remote mysteries, such as the vastness of the cosmos or the question of why the process of nuclear fusion, which takes place within a star, ever started in the beginning.

And yet the question of the nature of human beings is of such fundamental importance that it deserves much more attention than you currently give it, for only if you understand this will you start to get an idea of why the so-called "human condition" exists at all.

In order to start the process of understanding you must first of all go back to the start of everything – what your scientists call the Big Bang – for without that knowledge nothing makes any sense at all. What existed before the Big Bang? This is where your scientists cease to have ideas: they can be reasonably agreed on the state of the universe just after the event – in fact even micro-seconds after the event – but they cannot do anything but hazard guesses at the state of things prior to it. So what did exist – if anything existed at all? And if nothing existed, then what was the event which made it exist? Weighty questions indeed.

The simple answer is that the only thing which existed was ENERGY – for all your scientists agree that energy is indestructible. It can never be destroyed, although it can change its state, according to how it is used. So, it *must* have existed before the Big Bang, and it will continue to exist long after the universe has ceased to exist. But how does matter come out of energy? Once more, current scientific thought accepts that it is possible to create matter by using a large amount of energy, although the amount of energy needed to produce even one gram of matter is so large that it makes it prohibitively expensive to do more than a few laboratory experiments on the subject.

Also, the matter which is produced is of two different kinds: one is what you consider the normal kind, the stuff of which everything appears to be made – and you have known for a long time about the atoms and molecules which make up everything in your created world. The other is what you call "anti-matter", which is the exact reverse of matter – so opposed to it, in fact, that should one particle of matter meet one particle of anti-matter, there would be an enormous explosion, which would create ENERGY once more. In fact it would create exactly the same amount of energy that was needed to make the individual particles in the first place. This would then vindicate the postulate of one of your revered scientists, who formulated what you call the Law of Conservation of Energy, which is the empirical law of Physics.

It is interesting also to note that your cosmologists have now come to the conclusion that the only way to understand the mathematics of the universe is to accept that there is a vast amount of "dark matter" within it, which gives it the gravity which is needed to hold everything together – and we will be saying more about dark matter later on.

The truth is far more complicated than I have indicated so far, but yet these basic facts are indisputable. Energy produced matter, which is now widely spread throughout the universe, and in your own world everything which you consider to be substantial, which can be appreciated by one of the five senses, is composed of atoms. Each of these atoms can be further subdivided into smaller particles, each of which is kept by some force – or energy – in its own separate orbit within the atom – and this same thing applies whether or not the atoms are constituents of wood, metal, stone, water, or living tissue. Everything is connected – which is a very important principle of spiritual knowledge.

But however interesting all this may be, what has it to do with the fundamental nature of a human being? Well, the answer once more is fairly straightforward. Everything! The enormous power which existed before the Big Bang still existed after it, and still exists today, although in an altered state. It exists in every atom and molecule of Creation, and as every living creature is made up of atoms, that same power must exist in each of them. This may be difficult for human beings to comprehend – certainly those who are of a religious disposition, who may well be horrified at the thought of an animal being equated in any way to a human being – and yet it is so. Also – even more horrific – since everything in your world is composed of atoms of one kind or another, the primal energy in a piece of wood, a drop of water, or a stone is of the same kind as that in a human being.

Many decades ago your scientists found out what enormous energy lies within each atom, and have been able to unleash that same energy for many purposes. But is it not symptomatic of the human condition that the first major impetus towards understanding and controlling the use of that energy came because you wished to create weapons of such unbelievable power that they would obliterate the enemies of the countries which used them? Certainly, peaceful uses of the energy have since been discovered, but even now there are fears that those who wish to harm other states might get their hands on such weapons, and so trigger a war which could potentially destroy your planet, and change the structure of the galaxy within your universe.

* * *

I was saying that matter was created out of energy: it is possible to dispute what I have said by pointing out that the universe – or at least the one which you currently know – is so vast that there is an unimaginable amount of matter contained in it. So if a huge amount of energy is needed to produce even a small amount of matter, the total energy needed for the Big Bang would be so great that it would be simply inconceivable to a human mind. How can that be explained? Well, from our point of view the answer is, once more, simple: the amount of energy in Creation was, is and always will be infinite. The problem, from a human perspective, is the word "infinite" itself: infinity can be defined, but it can never be fully comprehended. For whatever you imagine it to be, it will be even greater, greater in size, greater in distance, greater in time – in fact, greater in every unit of measurement.

But do not be disheartened by the fact that you cannot understand the concept of infinite energy: just accept that it is beyond the power of the human mind – even the greatest mind – to understand, and in this you will come to the position where we are at the moment. Certainly we have more idea than you of what infinity is, but we have to accept our own limitations in that *we* will never be able to comprehend it fully. We accept that, whatever we may conceive as the ultimate, infinity is beyond that point – and if you do the same you will save yourselves much unnecessary mental gymnastics.

But this may ring a bell in the minds of those of you who are of a more religious disposition, for – putting aside the serious difficulties which you have in trying to reconcile your differences – your individual concept of the Supreme Power, understood by any name, is by definition a Being beyond all human understanding, infinite and all-powerful.

But let us move on a little further: the energy which comprises the universe is subject to certain fundamental metaphysical laws, some of which are not yet accepted by you. One of these laws is the Law of Attraction. You have known of specific applications of this law for some considerable time in your physical sciences: the force of Gravity, for example, has been accepted for centuries. Another is the attraction of atoms together to form the molecules which make up your known elements in Chemistry: this has formed the basis of your study of that science. But the Law of Attraction has a far wider significance than you currently understand: it applies in all aspects of life on your planet, from the reaction of so-called inert chemicals to each other, through the action of plants which instinctively seek light and nutrients for their own survival, and as far as the biological attraction between members of the human race itself. In every level of existence, in every way, this fundamental law manifests itself.

Some members of your species have known about these metaphysical laws for many millennia, and have used them to ensure their own survival, but as Humanity has become increasingly sophisticated the age-old knowledge has become progressively derided until now, in your "enlightened" age, it has become almost obliterated, and exists only in what you loftily dismiss as primitive tribes. But all is not yet lost. Increasing numbers of you are seeing that the present course of Humanity is taking it towards the physical extinction of a large proportion of the sentient creatures of your planet, and possibly towards the demise of the human race itself, and are trying to do something about the situation. Such people have become so alarmed by what is happening that they are increasingly turning back to seeking the old knowledge contained within the laws of Metaphysics, and are more open to accepting to look afresh at what was in former times accepted as traditional wisdom. This has led to a renewed interest in everything from alternative therapies and religious doctrines to changing lifestyles, and paradoxically also to the study of the belief systems of those primitive and aboriginal peoples who still exist. I say paradoxically, as the more remote or lost tribes are studied to see what benefit they may bring to the rest of Humanity, the more they are likely to be contaminated by contacts with modern society, which will lead eventually to the destruction of their own lifestyle.

***

Yet there is no need to travel to the most remote corners of the Earth to find lost tribes in order to start to understand how you, as a species, can start to turn away from your headlong rush to self-destruction. You have only to consider the few facts which I have already given to you, and make them the basis for your study. The problem is that your world is split into two different schools of thought – which we might call the Scientists and the Theologians. I am referring, of course, only to those of your species who actually *try* to understand the human condition, and not to the masses who just follow whatever their leaders tell them is the truth.

But many of you – members or former members of the masses – are now starting to be deeply unhappy at the current state of your society, and are finding that although you are surrounded with more and more physical comforts and material wealth, you are also becoming increasingly disillusioned with your life. This is so all over your planet, regardless of the local culture, and it is because you – as a species – are edging your way towards a realisation of what life *could* be like in an ideal society, where each individual achieves his or her true potential. You are also becoming aware of the yawning gap between what you call "the haves" and "the have-nots".

There was a time when Religion and Science were in harmony in your Western world. There were many clerics who were of a scientific mind, while all – or most – of your scientists were religious. But that changed when scientific discoveries came more into conflict with religious dogma, and eventually an uneasy truce was declared, in which it was accepted that all matters of a material nature were the province of Science, whereas matters of a non-physical nature, such as beliefs and speculation on the nature of human beings and on Creation itself were the province of Religion. And so it remained for many centuries. There were times when open rebellion broke out (for instance on the question of Evolution, which is still provoking controversy even today,) but by and large there was an acceptance of the existence – although not the validity – of the other school of thought.

But Science has progressed and Religion has developed – and paradoxically there is more common ground between them now than there has been for centuries. As your scientists make more and more discoveries, they are finding that many of their long-cherished concepts are not the immutable laws which they had once thought, and under certain conditions they are just plain wrong. So they are beginning to suspect that the laws of Science, which have been laid down and hallowed by observance over the centuries, can be over-ridden by higher laws of which they are only just becoming aware. This means that many scientists are now starting to talk in terms which would have been understood by religious sages who lived many centuries ago.

At the same time, those of you who are of a religious nature are also being influenced by changing attitudes. Many religions are becoming polarised, so that there is on the one hand a faction which is more ready to accept some of the findings of Science, and that is being balanced by an opposing faction which is becoming more literal in their interpretation of their religion. So currently you have the rise of what you call fundamentalism in religion, which is causing many of the current political problems in your world.

But for those Scientists and Theologians who are capable of moving towards the other school of thought, this is a time of immense opportunity, for it opens the way towards a true understanding of the fundamental nature of your species and how it fits into the overall scheme of things. So this is a very exciting time in the history of your planet, where members of the dominant species have the power to work together for the ultimate benefit of all of the planet's inhabitants – and in fact create a new and beautiful world.

Of course there will be many battles to be fought before the dawning of your new era – or what you call the "New Age" – and the extremists of both schools will continue to denounce those of the opposing side. But although the antagonism between opposing sides will inevitably continue, in the future this will be increasingly on the verbal level rather than the physical level. Then as time goes by more and more people will be attracted to the new knowledge which is being received, and the devastating conflicts which you are currently seeing in your world between different religious factions will become a thing of the past.

4. Energy and Intelligence

So let us now go back and try to sketch out what happened at the Big Bang. First, we must say that one of the fundamental processes of Creation – perhaps even the most important one of all – is that of Change. This means that everything, on every level, is continually in a state of flux, of movement and alteration. So nothing is ever permanent – even the basic energy of the universe. Energy can never be destroyed, only altered in state, but the alteration in its state is continuous, so that nothing is exactly the same from one moment of time to another. The ratio between the parts of the energy which are in a pure state and those which are in the state of matter is continually changing: there is a continuous ebb and flow between the two.

The fundamental Law of Change and Stability also ensures that nothing is ever the same as anything else, not only in space but also in time. The original impetus of Creation of any life-form was a *one-off*, and as you say, "Once the thing was made the mould was broken." This means that there is no duplication in the universe, nor can there ever be. You can of course see this phenomenon in your own human condition: no two human beings are ever the same. However similar they may be to outward appearances, there are always subtle differences which distinguish them. The many studies of identical twins which your scientists have carried out illustrate this. Despite the fact that many such twins, some of whom have been reared separately, have had remarkably parallel lives, there are always some differences. There has probably never been a case where the mother of identical twins has been completely unable to distinguish between them.

So the process of Change is always taking place, and when this happens over a long period of time in one species you have a development of that species – what can truly be called an evolution of the species. This may happen on a mental plane as well as on a physical plane, so that it is quite true to state that the intelligence level of the average human being is now far higher than it was some tens of thousands of years ago. But progress in one area of human life is usually balanced by regress in another: for instance, the power of instinct was very highly developed in the early stages of human life, and this was usually tied to self-preservation – quite simply, those who did not have it were not likely to survive for very long among the dangerous world of predators. But as human life has evolved over the millennia, this instinct has largely become dulled, as have the allied senses of smell, sight and hearing, because they have no longer been needed. Certainly, the situation is not the same among primitive peoples, but they tend to be rare exceptions to the general rule.

The phenomenon of Change applies on every level of being, from top to bottom. If you can imagine the state of affairs moments before the Big

Bang, there was a situation when the process of Change resulted in the Universe consisting of pure concentrated stable energy – which *had* to change. Here we use the word "Universe" to mean the totality of everything which then existed. And the only way that this energy could change was by creating matter and anti-matter, which it did in a gigantic explosion – the Big Bang. The force of the explosion created heat and light, which is the origin of the statement in many of your religious scriptures that there was initially darkness in the universe, and the Creator said "Let there be Light." We will expand on this theme later on.

* * *

I have mentioned the words "the Creator", and this will be understood by your Theologians, although not by your Scientists. This is because your Theologians have the image of the Creator as being some sublime Being and – because it is difficult for Humanity to conceive of a disembodied Creative Force – for some Theologians that meant that the Creator has to be thought of as in some way resembling a human being. In fact, in one of your holy scriptures it is stated that Man was made in the likeness and in the image of God – and so to followers of that religion it is obvious that God must be similar to a man in appearance. But from the point of view of your Scientists, the idea of crediting Creation to a personalized Being is plainly ridiculous, as they believe that everything which happened did so in a totally random way, so that the complete complexity of your universe and all its different component parts is merely the result of a series of accidents. Also, every life-form in your physical world is simply an evolution from one chance piece of protoplasm which came into being untold aeons of time ago. So perhaps in the future we would be on less contentious ground if, instead of using the word "Creator" we use the words "the Creative Force" – and let those on each side interpret that according to their own personal mindset.

So how can one reconcile these two opposing viewpoints, if it is indeed possible to do so? Alternatively, which one is right, and which one wrong? And can we say anything which will be acceptable to both sides?

Well, we are going to upset both sides by saying that each one is wrong, although paradoxically each one has some truth in its beliefs. For if I said that the Creative Force is pure energy, that will be generally accepted by Scientists, whereas if I said that the force is pure Intelligence, that would be generally accepted by many Theologians. But what if the original – and continuing – force behind Creation were Intelligent Energy? Both sides would, of course, dismiss the idea as pure nonsense, as neither would be able to understand the concept of Intelligent Energy – and yet in fact that is what the primary power behind Creation was, and what caused the original Big Bang.

* * *

And this is how the Big Bang came about: the primal intelligence wished to know itself, and so concentrated a part of its own Being – its own energy – in such a way and to such an extent that there *had* to be a reaction. Your scientists will understand the concept of action and reaction being equal and opposite, as this is one of your laws of Physics. It implies that the greater the action, the greater will be the reaction. And when *infinite* concentration – there is that word again – produces *infinite* pressure, the reaction will also be *infinite*. There came a point at which the force tending towards reaction overcame the force tending towards the concentration of the energy, and at that point there was an outburst of energy, of creative activity – or in other words, what you now know as the Big Bang. But before we go into a detailed analysis of this event, let us give you a little more information about your current understanding.

* * *

Over the millennia, your species has been edging towards an understanding of what life is all about, and how it began. You have sought to unravel the mysteries of the universe and at the same time the mysteries of the human condition. Because of the dictates of religion in your Western world, there came about the historic split between Religion and Science, and guidlelines were drawn up defining what was the province of Religion and what was the province of Science. But when you entered the new millennium, the distinctions between the two became more and more blurred, so that many of the things which your scientists are now exploring have become a bitter battleground for disputes which are reminiscent of those of four centuries ago.

At the same time that this has been happening, Time itself seems to be speeding up – and that is in fact true, as there are movements of energy across your galaxy of which you currently know little, which are not only affecting conditions on your planet but also – and very importantly – affecting each of you and your ability to relate to and understand your world. This has been happening gradually over the last two centuries, which in human terms is an extremely long time, but in galactic terms is only the twinkling of an eye. If you doubt this look back over the march of Science during the last century alone, and you will find that the majority of the material things which are so much part of your daily life today were either totally unknown or unavailable to the majority of the population one hundred years ago.
But of far more importance than the growth of knowledge is the effect that the process has had on your mentality. It has led to a polarisation of ideas, and this has in turn created some of the unfortunate manifestations of your current age. On the negative side it has led to the growth of fundamentalism and the unwillingness to accept the religious or scientific views of others. But on the positive side it has led to the opening of the minds of many of you – both

scientific and religious people – to the possibility that there is value in the views of others. This is an obvious paradox – that the same cause can lead to diametrically opposite effects – but it can be explained by the fact that you are all at different stages in your spiritual growth and understanding. Of course spiritual understanding has nothing at all to do with mental ability – there are many highly intelligent people on your earth who are mere babies in terms of spiritual understanding. And if many adults could take the time to listen to some of the things which children say, they would possibly find that there was a deep spiritual understanding in many of those ideas.

The pace at which life is evolving in your world is increasing rapidly, and if you look at the speed at which new scientific discoveries are being made you will see that the frontiers of Science are being continually pushed back – so much so that in many branches of Science what was mere conjecture only a few decades ago is now proven fact.

One of the areas of scientific knowledge which has come to the forefront of your consciousness over the last few years is what you call Quantum Mechanics, where your scientists have found that all matter is composed of minute particles of energy – called *quanta* – which seem to behave in a completely irrational way. They can appear and disappear at will, seem to have the ability to be in two places at the same time, and apparently can also communicate with other particles at a distance, without physical connections. What is more, the activity of these particles seems to be capable of being influenced by the thoughts of human beings who may well be several hundred miles from the site where the experiments are taking place. In fact, the behaviour of these particles in many instances seems to suggest that they might be guided by some form of intelligence.

Does this all sound vaguely familiar? If you are of a religious frame of mind, it is quite possible that it does, as for millennia human beings have believed in the power of thought to influence physical realities – for instance, by praying for the health of those who are sick, by remote viewing or by the laying on of hands in healing ceremonies. But the thought of some sort of intelligence governing the results of scientific experiments would be absolute anathema to the majority of scientists – it smacks too much of the concept of God – or a Supreme Being by some other name – and so cannot be considered.

But what if the particles themselves are not merely particles of energy – for matter is after all only one expression of energy – but also particles of *intelligent* energy – and are, in fact, *alive?* Could that explain some of the aspects of their behaviour which currently mystify your scientists?

In future, it will be realised that the idea of the existence of particles of intelligent energy, which today is at the utmost fringe of scientific possibility, is in fact only the *beginning* of the new understanding of the workings of the universe. And that may be seen as a first step towards the discovery of a Theory of Everything, which may lead to the Grand Unified Theory which scientists have been seeking for much of the last century.

But before we go into the subject much further, we have to tell you that when we use the word *particles* we are not meaning exactly the same as what you understand by the term. You have today identified many different types of particle, and have classified them all together as sub-atomic particles. We have to tell you that we are going back to a much lower level of complexity, to the primary particles which make up your universe. Those of which you speak are the results of what has happened when primary particles get *clumped together* in different configurations, and become something which takes on a separate identity. They are the amalgamation of several thousands – or even tens of thousands of primary particles – but naturally share many of their basic characteristics.

* * *

We have said that the whole universe is composed of energy, and that this energy is expressed in individual particles. We have also stated that each particle behaves in a way that suggests that it is a particle of *intelligent* energy, so now it is appropriate to consider the relation of the particles to each other.

First, let us say that the human concept of division is totally false. By division we mean that human beings understand everything as being separate: you are very fond of classifying things and putting them in their separate boxes. You talk of things being either animate or inanimate, of being plants, animals or humans, of being dead or alive, and so on. Yet in fact the truth is far more simple than that: the truth is that everything is connected at the most basic level – the level of particles – and so eventually there is no distinction whatsoever between any of the contents of your little boxes. The only difference is in the mode of expression of the particles. This idea needs a little expansion.

You already know of the association of like things, as it can be seen on many levels in your daily life. Animals, birds and fish gather together with others of the same species, and sometimes form large herds, flocks or shoals. Human beings also tend to associate with those of like mind, those who share an interest with them, who have the same hobbies, skills, pastimes or views. You even have in your language sayings which identify this as a fact of life, such as "Birds of a feather flock together." But until now few of you has got as far as identifying it as a Universal Truth, operating on the level of particles.

Let us imagine that a particle wishes to express itself as part of an inanimate object, for instance as part of an atom within a mineral. It would naturally become associated with an indefinite number – possibly millions – of other particles with the same aim and together they would form individual atoms which would in turn form the mineral. They would remain together for a certain length of time, after which they would disassociate themselves from each other. As the particles dispersed, the individual atoms would cease to exist as atoms, which would mean that the mineral would cease to exist in that precise form, and would change into something else.

While these particles are expressing themselves as atoms within a mineral, there would be others who would wish to express themselves as atoms within the cells of plants, trees, animals or even human beings. In all these cases, the same thing would apply, where the particles would remain together for a specified length of time and then would dissipate once more, so that the organism would go out of existence. Of course, in such cases the length of time when they were together would be considerably less than that for the particles in minerals – but the same principle would still apply.

So far we have spoken only about particles which express themselves in a *physical* form, as atoms of some substance which is known to, and measurable by, human beings. But what about those which have experienced all the possibilities of expression within physical atoms? If they wished to further their experience of life in your planet, they would have to express themselves in a non-physical way, as more directed forms of their own individual consciousness.

* * *

Now this is a phenomenon throughout your physical world, and of course for a long time you have been aware of the existence of atoms, and how they form part of everything in physical existence. The only new information here is the role that particles play in the constitution of the atoms – and the fact that the particles are themselves all specks of intelligent energy. But now let us take matters a little further and see what other manifestations the particles can produce.

Some of the particles which wish to *study* the *experience* of *being* an atom in a particular substance will combine with others with the same intention in order to form *units of consciousness*, which attach themselves loosely to the atoms in question. They act as observers only, and do not in any way interfere with the workings of the atom, for that would destroy the reason for forming the unit. But when the constituent particles of the physical atoms are dispersed and the atoms themselves go out of being, some of those constituent particles join those in the units of consciousness, which still remain in existence. They are joined by others which are similarly disassociated with the atoms which *they* have been observing, and eventually they form a *pool of consciousness* of the whole organism.

Exactly the same thing happens all the way up the evolutionary ladder of beings of increasing complexity. A particular type of organism will have individual cells composed of atoms made up of particles, and each of these atoms will have a unit of consciousness attached to it. Then, when the atoms combine to form a cell, the separate units of consciousness combine to form one single unit which now observes the cell. Cells in turn combine to make structures, which causes the observer units to combine in turn. The structures combine to make organisms, which then become more complex, until eventually something is produced which you are capable of classifying and putting into one of your little boxes, identifying it as a mineral, plant or animal – which has its own pool of consciousness.

If you have understood the scheme which we have outlined you will see that the more complex the organism is, the more complex will be the unit of consciousness which is attached to it. We do not use the word *size* in this context, for you understand size in three-dimensional terms, which are totally inappropriate to describe non-physical matters. Neither is the use of numbers appropriate, for the number of particles in a single cell is so astronomical that it is beyond the comprehension of most of you. So perhaps the only word which would be of any value in this context is the word *intensity*, and that is the word which we shall use: when we compare units of consciousness we will talk of their relative intensity.

So, you see that the greater the complexity of any organism the greater the intensity of its accompanying unit of consciousness, from the seemingly inert mineral ores, through the primitive forms of plant life and right up to the most complex of animal life-forms. You will also see that associated with each different organism and each life-form there has come into being a pool of consciousness.

* * *

Now we have to consider whether or not there is any sort of pattern in the movements of particles into and out of any of the individual atoms, cells, organisms or units of consciousness of which we have spoken, and we have to tell you that there is. At first sight it would seem that each of these particles is acting in a totally random way – at least it would appear like that to human eyes – but there is one factor which now intervenes to stop the total randomness. That factor is, as we have explained, that the particles are not just particles of energy, but particles of *intelligent* energy. They are suddenly introduced to a world which is composed of dense matter, so far removed from anything which they have experienced before that they are *curious* – to use a human term – and wish to experience the most alien thing about this new planet, which is the apparent inertia of the minerals which compose the planet itself. So their first experiences consist of being parts of the atoms of mineral ores – everything which you consider to be inanimate.

Following the experience of being part of an atom of each mineral, the natural progression for the particles is to band together to form a pool of consciousness for that particular mineral. An analogy in human terms might be that when people have been working in a particular job for a period of time they might get a promotion, which would allow them to view the workings of the department from a different – and higher – perspective, but also – crucially – to have more authority in how the department functions, and to be able from time to time to make suggestions on how it could be made to work more efficiently.

The particles continue to explore their new strange world by being part of each different mineral of the Earth in turn, and also being part of the pool of consciousness of that mineral, until after a period of hundreds of millions of years by your reckoning they have experienced everything about the structure of the planet itself. Then they turn to the next most foreign organism, becoming parts of the atoms of simple life-forms like single-cell plants. Now progress is relatively swift, as the life expectancy of such life-forms is dramatically shorter than that of minerals, and so they progress fairly rapidly through the whole range of plant life, up to the most complex of plant organisms.

But an interesting phenomenon occurs during this stage in their journey towards understanding everything about their new environment. We have said that the pools of consciousness are in some ways similar in function to the role of supervisors in your commercial companies: once the supervisor particles become associated with a particular plant, they are able to see where a change of plant activity might prove beneficial for that plant's eventual survival, and are able to *suggest* how changes might be made. But the big difference between the supervisor in a company and the supervisor particle is that the individual atoms of the plant are themselves made up of particles, which can be directly influenced on an energetic level in order to bring about beneficial changes. And since the life cycle of plant forms is so relatively short, a minute change brought about in each year of the life of the plant can have dramatic effects on the overall development of the plant – in fact, on its overall *evolution*.

* * *

Once more, the particles progress through the whole range of plant life on the planet, not only as constituent parts of plant atoms but also as constituents of the pools of consciousness connected with complete plants, until they know everything about all earthly plant life-forms. Next they come to the range of what you would consider more sentient beings, the animal kingdom, and here again there is a progression, starting with the simplest life-forms. The particles experience the fact of being part of the cellular structure of that form, and then – when the particular cell of which they are part disintegrates – become absorbed into a cellular unit of consciousness, before moving on to join with others to form a larger organism within the animal; there the same process is repeated, until the particle forms part of the pool of consciousness of the whole animal itself.

It is at this point that the supervisory role of which we have spoken really come into its own, as by this time the particles have experienced and understand all aspects of the physiology of the animal, and ways in which it could function more efficiently can be understood – so action can be initiated to introduce change on a physical level. This is a lot easier to do than you may expect, as it is a question of particles working to induce other particles to behave in slightly different ways. Naturally, the process produces only infinitesimal changes, but these changes, over an enormous period of time, all contribute to what you today call the "evolution of the species" which in your understanding means the process by which animal life gradually produced your race – homo sapiens.

5. Visitors from Space

Now Evolution is a very emotive word in human terms, but before I go on to speak about it I would like to tell you something about your planet itself. The initial point of Creation which you call the Big Bang took place many billions of years ago in human terms, and during that time an enormous number of life-forms have evolved, and are continuing to evolve. The vast majority of these life-forms do not have physical bodies in the way that you understand the word physical, but almost without exception their mental and spiritual bodies are far more advanced than you can currently comprehend. The majority of them have reached levels of technology which are beyond your wildest dreams, and some of your current long-term aims, such as space travel, have been known and practised by many civilisations for much longer than your species has even existed.

Your galaxy was formed many billions of years after the Big Bang, and within that galaxy your solar system is a junior component, so that when we consider your planet itself, it is in cosmological terms hardly into adulthood. But it is a relatively dense planet for the support of life-forms, contrary to what you currently believe, and this is what has made it so interesting to some of your close neighbours within your galaxy, who have been observing conditions here for many millions of years. From time to time you have had visits from denizens of other star systems, which have given rise to many of your most lasting myths and legends of "the gods" who came to create conditions for life to commence.

Have you ever thought that the similarity of these legends from widely differing parts of the world might be due to a basic grain of truth, which has been considerably distorted in the re-telling over the millennia? That truth is, of course, that from time to time you have been visited by beings whose powers were so much greater than those of the inhabitants of the time that they were considered as gods, and elaborate religious rituals were created in order to appease them and get them to bring fortunate conditions into the lives of human beings.

So far many of you have come to the same conclusion, and have attributed to such visitors the ability to advance the civilisation of the day by introducing new methods of communication, agriculture, social organisation, healing and many other disciplines. But I have to tell you that the visitors were of far more importance in the history of your race than you have ever imagined, as they were instrumental in the actual *creation* of the human race itself.

For more than a century there has been a battle raging in the realms of philosophy between the *Creationists* – usually religious people – who believe that your planet and all that it contains was created by some divine being, and the *Evolutionists* – usually scientists – who believe that everything happened through the forces of change and natural selection. So, to these scientists, humans evolved from early mammals, in shared ancestry with monkeys until eventually they became a separate species – homo sapiens.

May I now say something which is certain to upset both of the different sides in the argument once more: both are right, but yet paradoxically both are wrong. They are right in the fact that some of their ideas are correct, but wrong in denying totally the views of their opponents. For in truth your race was a mixture of evolutionary processes and creative actions. Let me explain what I mean:

You are well aware that there are scientists today in your world who are using your recent discoveries in the field of genetics to modify different organisms. This has led to furious debate about the wisdom of using genetically modified crops, while it has also led to the creation of *chimerae*, genetic crosses between two unrelated species which, while it occasionally happens in Nature, does so extremely rarely. But your scientists have now succeeded in creating an animal which is genetically a cross between a sheep and a goat, prompting various religious authorities to issue stark warnings about the dangers of "Man playing God."

But if you are capable of doing this, in your relatively early state of technology, can you not imagine a situation where a highly advanced civilisation from a distant part of the galaxy could, through genetic manipulation, experiment in modifying the life-forms on your planet over many million years in order to create the human race? For this is what in fact happened.

Of course, in the process of what we may call *the human experiment* there were many mistakes made. Anyone who has been involved in scientific research will understand that there are as many false starts experienced as there are outright successes. But even these mistakes, these dead-end avenues of research, are documented in parts of your mythology, stories of one-eyed giants, of creatures that were half-human and half-animal, or a mixture of two different animal species. Once more, myths and legends rarely spring up out of the imagination of an individual: more often they are based on some original facts, which then become modified or distorted over a long period of re-telling.

Yet there came a time when the direct experimental modification of the genetic material came to an end, and that was when the element of rational consciousness had been introduced into the human being. At that point there were those among the alien scientists who realised that they had gone far enough in their experiments: an analogy in your modern-day world is that you are now able to create a human foetus through cloning, but to do so would raise such a storm of international protest that no one would ever dare to do it.

Long before this time the component of emotion, which in animals is found only as simple instinct, had already been greatly enhanced. But that had been the *relatively* simple part of the experiments – after all, it is not too difficult to enhance something which already exists, albeit in a fairly primitive form. The far more complex part of the experiments lay in the grafting on to the basic animal – for that was what it was at that time – a higher level of consciousness, of which the main constituent was the element of rational thought.

So the new species was planned to have three separate identifiable facets, which for sake of a name we will call *bodies* – a physical body, an emotional body and a rational – or mental – body. But when we recall the fact that all matter throughout the universe is composed of individual particles of intelligent energy, and energy is of course eternal, the fourth component of a human being was the link to his/her eternal power-source, the particles of primary energy from which he/she was originally formed. This has been given many names in various cultures but we shall refer to it as *spirit*, and so the fourth component of a human being was a spiritual body.

Of course this took aeons of time to achieve, and this summary I have greatly condensed the whole process. I will not elaborate on the millennia of experiments which preceded the final production of your species, nor on the thousands of dead-ends which were experienced before success was finally achieved, but I will mention one small technical detail which will be useful at a later stage to help you to understand the current composition of your being. For a long time the scientists were trying to start with the original physical matter and graft onto it the less dense material, which was to create the emotional body, until eventually they realised that it could not be done – they were starting at the wrong end of the process. They had to start with the lightest – finest – material and then gradually find ways of attaching the more dense layers to it, until eventually what they had created could be attached to a physical body of flesh.

If you have two materials which are of a different, non-compatible, composition and you are trying to attach them together in a way which does not destroy either of them, then the only way to do it is to create an interface of a third material which can be attached to both of the others – and this is exactly what finally had to be done at each stage of the process. The first thing that happened was that some particles of pure energy were attached to a medium which acted as a kind of blueprint of a level of concentrated consciousness, and this was then attached to the consciousness itself – the mental body. Then the process was repeated, and a denser blueprint was attached, which led to the next level, that of concentrated emotion – the emotional body. Then the last blueprint – of the physical body – was attached and the whole assemblage was joined to a body of flesh.

The final result was that the newly created being was composed of seven layers, each being formed of particles in a progressively denser form until the final manifestation of a human being in a physical body. It is important to grasp this basic principle, as it is the foundation of much of the information that is given later on.

* * *

Many readers of this book may be shocked by the whole concept that your species was the result of a series of genetic experiments, but this can be put into perspective by considering two things:

First, that even in your present society you are daily conducting experiments on various forms of life in order to improve them in one way or another. Indeed, much of your current food consists of animals or plants which have been created through a process of selection over a long period of time. Granted, until relatively recent times you have been selecting merely on the basis of noticing the physical properties of the plant or animal in question and breeding in order to enhance those desirable factors, and to create a greater yield of food. Yet now, due to your level of technological expertise, you can start to work on a more fundamental level of experimentation – which you call *genetic modification*.

But less understandable are the breeding experiments which have so deformed the original root stock of particular animals that they have caused suffering to the animal in question, or have ensured that it lives out its life in considerably more miserable conditions than it would have normally done in its wild habitat. Examples which come to mind are of breeding different forms of poultry which are so large that they can hardly stand upright for any length of time, let alone walk or run around as they would normally do, or of farming animals, fish or birds in such conditions that they are prey to diseases which can only be controlled by regular medication.

Many of the things which have been – or are still being – done can be condoned by you as being essential for the production of food for your sustenance, but you have also had breeding programmes which have produced animals, birds or fish which have exaggerated physical characteristics, purely so they can be kept as pets and admired. Many of these programmes have produced pets which may seem to be very physically attractive but which have either increased susceptibility to disease or illness, or which have a shortened life expectancy.

Possibly the least understandable of all to an impartial observer is your tendency to think of other *lower* life-forms as merely material on which to experiment to produce new drugs or cosmetics for your race. Fortunately, there are those among you who now believe that this is unacceptable, but so far they are in the minority. There are also many people who are against using animals, fish or bird products as food, preferring to eat only from vegetable sources, on the grounds that they do not wish to eat the flesh of sentient animals. But it is possible that such people would be offended if we suggested that on a basic level all life-forms are created from intelligent matter and so all life-forms are sentient.

The second thing to consider is that everything which was done to modify the characteristics of your primeval ancestors was done with the intention of *helping* to create a species on your planet which would have the capacity to understand and to work *consciously* with the forces which are inherent in the working of the universe. In fact all was done in total altruism – a wish to do *good* without consideration of selfish gain. I realise that this is a foreign concept to many of your race, who believe that the only happiness in life is to be able to be better, more powerful, more clever or richer than everyone else. But such altruism – I would call it *Love*, were it not for the fact that the word has been so totally debased in your current society that it no longer has any of its true meaning – is one of the indicators of the degree of development of all civilisations throughout the universe.

The final reason for the creation of your race – which we have called *the human experiment* – was so that through you all other life-forms on your planet could be provided with a developmental ladder back to their cosmic origins – something which we will return to later on.

To sum up:

1. All life-forms are created from the same particles,

2. expressed at different levels of density,

3. so all life is essentially interconnected.

This is something that most human beings will find very difficult to understand.

* * *

Just to return for a short time to those original experiments: consider for a moment the level of technical expertise which was displayed by those alien scientists in order to produce the level of complexity which makes up an individual human being. Your scientists are currently just at the beginning of their discoveries about the sub-atomic particles which make up the universe, and have only recently reached the stage of being able to prove that they even exist. But those scientists working in that *original* project were not only *aware* of the particles, but could also *use* them and modify their behaviour in certain ways to bring them together at the different levels of density of which we have spoken earlier. In addition, they were also able to *bind* them together so that they can disassociate from each other only under strictly defined conditions.

The discerning reader may query the use of the *present* tense in the last sentence, as the experiments were done so long ago. The reason is quite simple: the structure which was set in place all those many aeons ago *still exists*, and when this is understood completely it will provide answers to many long-standing questions about the human condition. Such questions include definitions of the moments when a human life begins and when it ends, and questions about whether there is any form of existence before or after the life of a human being on your planet, or about the mechanism which makes it possible for emotional disturbances to have an effect on physical health.

* * *

Now this is the point at which we have to mention the fact that in the Universe as a whole – the totality of all of Creation – there are many different universes, and your reality exists in only one of those universes. Your scientists have already postulated that there could be mathematically at least eleven different universes, and they are rapidly approaching the truth here, as there are actually thirteen. So they have come a long way from their position of fifty years ago, when the idea of the existence of more than one universe would have been ridiculed as a science-fiction fantasy. Also, in each universe there are a range of different dimensions. But what do the words *another dimension* mean? Quite simply, it means that as all matter consists of different sets of vibrations – something which you already know – a different dimension to yours exists when those vibrations are stepped up by such a large factor that everything which exists in it can no longer be perceived by any of the instruments which are currently in use in your science.

Human beings have their senses attuned to a certain range of vibrations, and so they cannot recognise anything beyond that range – it simply does not appear to exist. But other species on your planet have senses tuned to different frequencies, and are able to recognise signals which are emitted at those frequencies. Dogs, for instance, have a much wider range of hearing than human beings, a fact which is used in dog whistles, which operate on frequencies beyond human hearing, but are still recognisable to dogs. Bats use a very sophisticated form of radar to locate their prey at night, and whales and dolphins can communicate with each other over long distances through using very low frequencies of sound. Many insects have the ability to sense ultra-violet light, and Nature is full of examples of similar phenomena – we are sure that you can think of many others.

Now in your science you currently have some very sophisticated instruments, and yet they are capable of only touching at the edges of other dimensions. Could you imagine a system where everything which exists does so at the frequencies experienced in your world multiplied by a factor of 1,000,000? Of course not – and yet such systems do exist. Now the reason that you cannot see sub-atomic particles for more that a minute fraction of a second is because they are moving and vibrating at very high speeds, and are moving backwards and forwards through several dimensions, appearing in each for only a relatively short time – the relativity concerns the rate of the vibration of the overall system through which they are passing. So, if they pass through a system which has a high vibrational rate, relative to your own, it means that they will stay there for longer than they would in your system.

Some of your scientists have made great progress in understanding the meaning of *time*, and have rightly associated it with speed, and in particular with the speed of light. But it will open a completely new field of research for them if they consider a different dimension of being where the vibrational rate is so elevated that even the speed of light in your universe is considered as slow. Then they would get an insight into how the same particle can appear in two different places at the same time, a fact which is currently baffling them.

But to go back to those alien scientists we have been considering, the reason why they were able to do such advanced research into particles, and modify the behaviour of these to such an extent that they became like simple building blocks, is that *they themselves* were able to move in and out of higher dimensional systems with ease. But the really clever part was to be able to join together material of a higher vibrational rate, which they had been able to manipulate with ease in a higher dimension, to the far denser physical material of your own planet.

But what is the relevance of all this to you at this present point in your evolution? Well, quite simply, it is that everything connected with a human being which is not of the physical body can exist on only a temporary basis in your world. The discarnate consciousness – the pool of consciousness of humanity – the pools from which the mental and emotional bodies are formed, and those separate pools from which the interfaces or blueprints of which we have spoken earlier are created, can exist only in other – higher – dimensions. So only a small part of you – each one of you – is naturally at home in your present planet. The far greater part of you is more accustomed to an existence in a higher dimension – and actually spends more time in that dimension – something we will return to later on.

6. Planetary Influences and Astrology

So let us try to put together a few of the things of which we have spoken so that we can show how a human being is created. We have explained how all matter is made up of particles, which come together to create atoms, then molecules, then cells, and so on until complex structures are formed – the most complex of which is, of course, your own species. We have said that there is a continuous progression of particles up the chain of complexity, starting from the most basic inanimate level of mineral ores, and continuing through single-celled creatures, plants and animals. At each level within any organism the particles first experience existence in a physical form, and then pass into the unit of consciousness of that level. They then progress to higher levels until they experience existence in the complete organism, and its pool of consciousness. Having spent some time – and *time* in this context may mean many millennia – in learning everything about all organisms at that stage they then migrate to an existence in a physical form at the lowest level of the next level of complexity.

So eventually, we reach the stage where a large group of particles have bunched together and now form the pool of consciousness of your own species, homo sapiens. Every particle in this group has passed through all the stages of physical manifestation on your planet, and also has been part of every pool of consciousness. It has also been part of physical organisms within human bodies and their associated units of consciousness. Now only one last hurdle remains before it has experienced *everything* connected with the planet, and can proceed to other experiences on other planets, or in other systems. The final hurdle? The experience of *being* a conscious member of your species.

So, at an *appropriate* time – which will be explained later – a group of particles splits itself off from the main pool of consciousness and starts the process which was devised and laid down so many aeons ago by those alien scientists. Working as one entity, the group of particles – or for ease of expression we will say *it* – starts by clothing itself in a layer of the first interface material, which allows it to fuse with the particles which have been engineered to form mental consciousness – the mental body. Then it takes on a denser protective layer, which it needs in order to fuse with the much coarser emotional body. Then finally, it is ready to take on the third protective layer – denser still – which will provide the final interface and allow fusion with physical body.

So far, the process has been relatively simple and straightforward, as the original entity has been working with particles which – although being at different levels of density – are still recognisable as particles. But the difficult stage now lies ahead, that of fusing with particles which are acting out their own existence as individual cells in a physical body – and which provide a totally different level of challenge.

The first part of that challenge is in the selection of a foetus with which to fuse. In fact, as this is the first time that the entity has tried to become a human being, it is not really correct to talk of selection at all – the process is totally random. At any one time there are hundreds of millions of women who are pregnant in your world, and the entity gravitates to one of these, enters the womb and starts the process of integrating with the foetus. The process itself is extremely complex, and takes many months to complete. It involves *forming a duplicate* – the final interface – of all the parts of the physical body out of the material of the emotional body, and finally attaching that duplicate body to the physical body by means of an umbilical cord – similar in form and function to the physical umbilical cord through which the expectant mother feeds the foetus which it is in the womb. Some of the more religious-minded of you will recognise this umbilical cord as something which you know as the *silver cord*.

So finally, the baby is born, and it is composed of several different bodies – only one of which is visible to the human eye. But all of these bodies are *part of* the child, so that the particles which compose them are no longer able to act independently of the physical body – and certainly cannot remember what they were or where they came from. The only thing which can do that is the original entity – group of particles – which started off the whole process, and which is now – paradoxically – destined to take a back seat and become a mere observer during the life of the new human being.

* * *

Let us now address the question of an *appropriate* time: in order to do this we have to remind you that everything in your universe is connected to everything else on the level of particles, for all particles resonate with each other. Your scientists have proved this by doing separate experiments in which particles in one location have been able to influence the behaviour of others on the opposite side of the world. What is more, they have been influenced *at the same time as the experiment*.

But why stop when you consider the behaviour of particles within the confines of your planet? For exactly the same rules apply on the level of your solar system, galactic system and universal system. For so long your scientists have been measuring the distance of everything within your known universe in terms of the speed of light, so that the distance of remote galaxies from you are expressed in tens, hundreds or thousands of light-years. So the energies of these remote bodies cannot conceivably have a noticeable effect on you and your current civilisation – but if it is possible to consider such energies on a particle level, then there could be a very noticeable effect indeed.

But for the moment let us stay within your solar system, and consider how your planet is affected by other celestial bodies within the system. First of all we have to consider the sun itself, for without the sun no life on your planet would be able to exist in any form that you would recognise as existence. It provides heat and light, the two most important things in

a) regulating the temperature of the planet at a level where the life-forms are able to exist and
b) providing the basic energy to start the food chain on which all higher life-forms depend.

But it does much more than that: it provides a constant stream of magnetic energy which, by resonance, affects the planet itself, setting up lines of force in a grid pattern and turning the whole planet into a gigantic sounding device, capable of receiving signals from other celestial bodies within your system and beyond. And it is this grid system which has such a great effect on the behaviour of so many of the life-forms on Earth – including your own species – for it is the switching magnetic polarities of the sun's emissions which give the stimulus for the foetus within the womb to eventually make its entry into the world. This is a field of study which has already been explored by some of your more inspired scientists, and it could well occupy the attentions of more of your orthodox medical researchers.

As for other aspects of the grid, many of the species on earth are able to tune in to the lines of force, and use them for navigation over long distances. Examples of this are many and varied, from the migration of eels and salmon back to the spawning grounds which were the original places where they started life, to the annual migration of large herds of animals to new pastures and the migration of vast flocks of birds. All use what you class as instinct in order to make their journeys, but in fact they are using primeval senses in order to locate themselves, senses which have largely been lost by human beings.

Human beings have lost many of the innate instinctive abilities which their remote ancestors had. To compensate in part for this they have now reached a level of technological skill that enables them to place instruments in orbit round the planet, beaming signals back and telling them exactly where they are at any one time – but in doing so they are merely mirroring skills which more primitive life-forms have been using instinctively for millennia!

* * *

In general, the more that your species has evolved, the more it has developed and relied on mental skills in order to manage the challenges of everyday living, and the more that this has been done, the more you have moved towards a materialistic view of life, and divorced yourselves from your connection with your essential nature and your instinctual skills. There are, of course, exceptions to this general rule: there are still tribes in remote areas whose life-style has not changed much over the millennia, and there are also indigenous peoples in certain parts of the world who still retain much of the original lore of the old times, but in general their knowledge is derided and scorned by most in your modern society. Historically, also, those who did not follow orthodox religious beliefs at many times in your past were likely to be persecuted and even slaughtered by the more "enlightened" religious zealots of the time.

But all is not lost: in your world, currently, there is a growing realisation that the greatest threat to the survival of many of the species on the planet – your own included – is the sort of life-style of waste and destruction which a large proportion of your fellow human beings are leading. This has led to a resurgence of interest in the study of those who live in harmony with the planet, a move towards *greener* living, and a growing awareness that human beings have so many innate skills which are never used. It has been said, for instance, that the average human being never uses more than ten per cent of the capacity of his/ her mind: we would put it at a far lower figure than that.

We were pointing out the effects which celestial bodies have on your planet, and we have mentioned the most obvious ones – those generated by the sun. But almost as evident are those caused by the moon, for it is the nearest neighbour of the Earth, and so can hardly be unnoticed by any human being. The moon has a massive effect on the physical structure of your planet, as by the force of attraction – of which you know the physical laws – it causes the tides in your seas. It is less known that it also causes tides within the land-mass, and there is a specialist branch of knowledge in agriculture which accepts that the moon has a subtle – yet recognisable – effect in the timing of plant growth.

What is much less known is the way that the moon can affect the fertility cycles of women, and indeed, combined with the sun it can decide the level of fertility of an individual woman, or even condemn a woman to being barren. This was, of course, before the days of your creation and use of fertility drugs, which have changed the lives of so many women and enabled them to become mothers, when Nature was denying this. But of course you are now starting to recognise some of the dangers inherent in this.

Even less understood is the way in which the moon has an effect on the mind and emotions – although for many centuries abnormal mental behaviour has been associated with the moon – you even have the word *lunatic* to describe someone who is insane.

But both the sun and the moon are very large and very obvious bodies when seen from the surface of your planet. What about the other celestial bodies, planets and asteroids in the solar system? Do they also have any effect on your earth? Yes indeed, but the size of the effect has been vastly underestimated by your scientists, who once more apply the Law of Gravity to show that the effects on the Earth of the planets are so small as to be virtually negligible. Not so! First of all, each of these bodies is held within the sun's own gravitational field, and their different positions within that field create stresses within the sun itself, which then give rise to various solar phenomena, such as sunspots and solar flares – both of which certainly have an effect on your planet. In fact, if you consider the whole solar system as one single organism which is constantly changing, then you realise that the Earth, being part of that organism, must also be affected by the changes.

But it is not only indirectly that the other celestial bodies in the solar system affect the Earth, for each one has its own characteristics derived from its age, density and the types of life-form which it contains. We remind you that all manifestations of Creation, being based on the same primary particles of intelligent energy as those in your planet, can be considered as life-forms – although you may not yet be able to perceive them as such. The emanations of each of the celestial bodies also react on a particle level with the particles of your own planet, and with the particles within each of its life-forms – including your own. So the whole picture is certainly far more complex than most of you currently imagine, as you are being continually influenced by each of the celestial bodies within the overall organism which is the solar system itself. And since that picture is constantly changing, no single moment of time has ever duplicated the influences of any previous time, nor will it before the whole of your planet eventually ceases to exist.

So what does that mean on a human level? It means that the overall pattern of influences at the moment of your birth was unique – and so you were – and still are – unique. And the *appropriate time* which I have mentioned was the time at which the particles within you reacted with the emanations of the whole solar system in order to give the foetus the initial stimulus to start the process of its own birth. Your medical scientists realised many years ago that the timing of the birth labour came from the foetus itself. The greatest influence was, of course, the sun and its changing magnetic field, but the influences of the moon and the other bodies combined to make the *right* time for your birth.

* * *

In the case of the Western tradition of Astrology, observations have been made over a period of almost five thousand years in order to arrive at the current understanding. But scientists doubt the present explanation of how it all works, due to what you call *the precession of the equinoxes*; so they have concluded that the whole subject of Astrology is rubbish, and in arriving at this conclusion they have at a stroke discarded five millennia of observations. This is faulty reasoning. It is the *explanation* which is at fault, not the basic system, and perhaps if the scientists and astrologers could agree to discuss the subject together they might arrive at a closer understanding of the whole process.

But astrologers are also at fault in not taking account of scientific fact, and in trying to use the basic techniques handed down through the centuries without updating them with reference to current astronomical data.

Let us try to shed a little light on the whole subject by pointing out what has already happened in this study, and see if we can indicate further avenues of research for those who want to find out the whole truth of the matter. We will speak only of the Western astrological tradition, as astrology in the East has followed a different course.

The first formalised study of Astrology took place in the area which you now know as Iraq almost five thousand years ago, and at that time the Sun, viewed from the Earth, was seen to be against the constellation of Aries at the time of the Spring equinox, so that is the fundamental base on which your astrological philosophy is founded.

But after two thousand or so years of study, the Sun – viewed from the Earth – had entered the preceding sign, Pisces, and so all the information which had been gleaned up to that date *should* have been re-evalued in order to take that fact into account. The Sun and all its planets were now working in the same way as before, but *in a different mode* – and this fact was never realised. Now, more than two thousand years later, the same thing has occurred, with the Sun being poised to move into Aquarius, when once more the *mode of operation* will change. So what your astrologers need to do is to study the way in which whole system is now going to work, and to start to apply the modifications.

Now why is this so important? Is it worth laying so much stress on what is – at most – an interesting diversion for so many people who follow their stars in your daily journals and in magazines? The answer must be a resounding "Yes!" When you really understand what is happening to the human race you will realise that Astrology plays a vital part in the whole process of human existence, and that without it a large piece in the complex picture of how and why things happen as they do would be completely missing.

* * *

We mentioned that you are constantly being bombarded with influences from within your solar system, and have pointed out that, as the configuration of celestial bodies within the system are constantly changing, every moment provides a snapshot of a unique set of influences, which can never be repeated. So the moment of birth is of great importance, and indeed, this fact has been known to your astrologers for millennia. But there are other moments in the formation of the foetus which are also important: the moment of the initial ejaculation of male sperm in the process of intercourse is also of great importance in the life of the physical body of the foetus, and the moment of the implantation of the subtle bodies – the mental and emotional bodies and their respective interfaces – into the womb, which we have described earlier, is also important. Each of the three moments carries the mark of a particular point in time, and the interaction of the three points in time is of prime importance to the formation of the eventual human being.

You will note that we have not mentioned the moment of implantation of the fertilised ovum into the lining of the womb. This is obviously important, but from the point of view of the creative activity, it is the moment of ejaculation, which symbolically represents the primal outpouring of the original act of Creation, which is of the greater importance. If – or *when* – human beings recognise the effect that the ambient conditions at the time of intercourse have upon the formation of the future foetus and its later development, they will not treat the sexual act in such a casual manner.

* * *

Your scientists have reached the point at which they are able to create a foetus by joining male sperm and a female ovum in a laboratory, and then implanting it in the mother's womb, and they have been surprised by how many failures there are in the process. May we suggest a possible reason? In the natural way, through sexual intercourse, the cosmic conditions at the time are the same for the male and female. When sperm is taken from a donor, the moment of ejaculation can be weeks, months or even years before the attempt at impregnation, and so the cosmic conditions are almost certain to be totally different. Possibly if this fact is recognised and an attempt is made to synchronise the moment that the sperm is produced a little more closely with the attempted impregnation, your scientists will have a considerably higher success rate.

* * *

So far we have mentioned only the influences from within the solar system which affect the Earth, but when we look at those external to it we see that there is much more scope for you to be affected. The main difference is that those outside influences act over very long periods of time, and so have a generational, centennial or even millennial effect on humanity. You already have terms within your dictionary defining *Ages* – e.g. the Bronze Age, Iron Age, Dark Ages, Middle Ages, Industrial Age, Nuclear Age, and so on, and you understand these terms, although you would be hard pressed to define a precise date for the beginning or end of any of them. In fact their timing was largely influenced by different alignments of celestial bodies within your galaxy. Of these, the most potent is the movement of the Sun against the background of the constellations, which we have mentioned previously.

Now by analogy, the entry of the sun into a new constellation is similar to the entry of a new life into your world – although it cannot be fixed with such accuracy – and so is a most important occurrence. Such a situation is what you are currently experiencing, and it is a very interesting time for you. Indeed, combined with the fact that there are several unusual line-ups across your galaxy which are affecting your solar system at this same time, it is not an exaggeration to say that this could be a turning point in the history of your species.

In conclusion, may we remind you that:

1. you are an integral part of your planet and of every life-form on it,

2. your planet is an integral part of the solar system, which is an integral part of your galaxy – and so on, until everything is eventually part of the totality of Creation.

3. So you, at a fundamental level, are a part of everything in Creation and interact with it – which sets the scene for our later discussions.

7. Kali Yuga and the Rise of Numan

As I have mentioned previously, the entry of the Sun into another constellation is of great significance, not just for individual human beings – or even for the human race – but also for the evolution of all life-forms on your planet. The energy of change is so strong that it excites all life-forms in each of the different levels of existence – mineral, plant and animal – and causes an urge to move on. In most cases this is a relatively unimportant move, for instance from one plant species to another, but for a large number of particles, which have reached the end of their possible experiences on one particular level, it is the trigger to move up the evolutionary ladder to the next higher level – e.g. from mineral to plant, or from plant to animal. Of course, in most cases such movements would never be noticeable to a human being, but there is one movement which is certainly significant – and that is the movement between animal and human.

Consider the situation of an particle which has risen through all levels of the ladder until it reached the end of its experience on the animal level, and then started its experience in human flesh, first on a cellular level then on increasing levels of complexity until finally it becomes part of an entity which is a *conscious* human being *for the first time*. Now, suddenly, the entity is a completely independent individual, something which it has not been since the last time that it was an animal, and not only that, it now has mental and emotional faculties which it did not then have. But it does not have any background of ethical or moral principles to guide it, so it is more likely to react to situations which it faces in a similar way to what it did during its last – animal – life. Is it any wonder that the final years of the age which is ending – in your present case the final years of the Age of Pisces – have always been noted as periods of great upheaval, when all kinds of excesses of behaviour have been shown. In the tradition of one of your major religions, this period is called Kali Yuga, the Age of Destruction.

If you look around your present world, you will see so many of these upheavals taking place at the moment, not only at the world level, but also in national, local and personal scenarios. There is turmoil everywhere, and the rate of change of everything seems to be accelerating for all of you. At the same time that you are marvelling at the speed of scientific development and the growth of technological expertise, you are progressively more appalled at the horrific acts of cruelty which you see reported in your daily news bulletins, and you ask yourself how the perpetrators can behave so much like animals. Yet the explanation is so simple: they behave like animals because – essentially – they still are.

Let me give you an example of this: in recent years there has arisen a phenomenon in your society of large gangs of individuals roaming around and picking on unsuspecting – and innocent – individuals, attacking them and in some cases even killing them. Such gangs have later boasted about what they have done, and when prosecuted in the courts have not even shown the slightest sense of regret or remorse.

The reason for this is that most of the members of these gangs are complete human beings for the first time in their existence, and that the previous time they were whole individuals was when they were members of a feral pack of animals, so they are now behaving in a similar way. The big difference between their present behaviour and their previous behaviour is that then they were acting purely on an instinctive level, and killing out of a need for food, whereas now on a mental level they can see the action of hunting as a pleasurable occupation in its own right.

You may well argue that such individual acts of cruelty have been evident over many years; indeed, during the last World War which engulfed the majority of the nations on your planet, there were horrific acts of cruelty, even attempted genocide, and similar situations have been repeated several times in more recent times. But such facts do not destroy the explanation which I am putting forward, they merely extend the timeline back several decades. For of course there is no exact date for the Sun to enter a new constellation, and so the ambivalent influences which occur during the period of change are felt over a hundred or more of earth years. But within a short space of time you will reach the end of this transitional period and things will start to settle down once more.

But you may still ask, "Why are we so aware of all this happening now, when we weren't before?" Once more, the answer is fairly simple. There is only a relatively short space of time during which an entity may progress from one level of existence to another, and as more and more entities crowd in – to beat the deadline – the overall process of assimilation for the new humans comes under stress, and the temporary anomalies are more easily recognised. There is a mechanism for helping new humans to be absorbed, which I will now describe to you.

* * *

In your world you are well aware of the law which states that action and reaction are equal and opposite, which means that as one force acts on another, the second reacts on the first in the same way. To give a rather mundane example, if you were running at a certain speed and ran into a tree, the effect on your body would be exactly the same — and equally harmful – as if the tree had travelled towards you and hit you. But what you do not yet understand is that this is merely the earthly manifestation of a much more fundamental law – in fact the prime law which affects all Creation – that of Cause and Effect.

For everything which happens has a cause, and every cause will have an effect.

Now on a level of basic particles, the fact that Cause and Effect are linked can be seen instantly, as they both happen at the same time. But in life upon your planet things are very different, and this difference is the result of the difference in the vibrational level of physical matter. Remember what we said previously, that the difference between the vibrational rates of the *primary* particles and of particles which are bound together to a density which can produce physical matter is very great indeed – so great that there is a need to insert interfaces between the different bodies in a human being in order to allow them to even remain in contact with each other.

And so we come back to the animal which has his first experience as a human being. He has all the appropriate faculties, has the new ability to reason, and also has the new sensation of emotions, which is a much heightened form of his previous animal instincts. But he has no knowledge or understanding of *right and wrong*, of what is acceptable or desirable, or of what consequences certain of his actions will produce.

He finds that certain actions bring him pleasure, while others bring pain, and he is not too concerned if actions which bring him pleasure are at the same time bringing pain to others. But what he does not realise is that preceding every action which he takes there is a thought; that each thought then creates a vibration, and then *that* vibration, added to all the other vibrations which he has already created during his life, will create an energy field round him. And since energy is indestructible that energy field, once created, will remain in force until it is neutralised by another energy field *of equal force and in the opposite direction.*

Sooner or later this new human being will cease to exist as a separate entity – or as you say will *die* – but that is not the end of the matter, for something which has not happened previously will now come into effect. In previous – animal – existences, the animal had no mental and emotional bodies, since these were all part of the genetic engineering which went into the original creation of the human being. All that it had was a single interface to allow the instinctive body to join to the physical cells, so that soon after physical death there was nothing left of the animal at all: the particles which made up the physical body had disintegrated, as had most of those in the instinctive body; a few particles had joined the pool of consciousness of the animal species, but the remainder were now free.

But in this new situation, during the course of his life the new human – let us give him a name to identify him, and call him Numan – had produced this separate field of energy *which had been attached to his mental and emotional bodies.* Although the physical body – and with it its interface – would disintegrate, those others could not, and so remained in being. Soon after the moment of physical death, the cells of the physical body began to disintegrate, releasing their atoms and the particles which they contained. Next, the interface between the emotional and the physical body – which was no longer needed – also dissolved, releasing the particles at that level as well. But there the process stopped, for the emotional and mental bodies, complete with their respective interfaces, were now bound together by the energy field, and so indissoluble, and the original particles which had brought them into being were now imprisoned and could not be released *until the energy field which bound those bodies together had been neutralised.* And so Numan had started his journey through the human condition.

Author's note: *This gives an explanation of what is normally known as Karma, and is considered in more detail later in the book.*

* * *

This pattern continued over many earthly lives, with the directing particles choosing at random a foetus in which to be born, and with Numan acting out of basic instinct, using his mind to make deliberate decisions about which actions to take, based on whether the immediate results were pleasant or not, and with no thought for the results of his actions on other human beings. And increasingly the energy field which had been created round the mental and emotional bodies became stronger, until it reached a critical point where it *had* to be discharged.

You are aware of the phenomenon of lightning, where an electrical charge builds up in the clouds and, at the same time the opposite charge builds up on the earth beneath. Then, when a critical point is reached, the tension between the two masses of electrical force becomes so great that they reach out to each other, and a bridge between the clouds and the earth is created for a fraction of a second, and allows both charges to neutralise each other.

This is a similar phenomenon to what happens in human life, and so the next phase of Numan's existence starts – one which will remain with him for the rest of his time on Earth. For the next time that he is ready to enter into a foetus, he will be attracted to a time and a place in which the overall influences of the solar and galactic bodies will create a situation which has the potential to bring him experiences *which will neutralise a part of the energy field which has been built up over many lives.* This is what we referred to when we earlier used the phrase *an appropriate time.*

So when he starts his new life on Earth, he will now begin to have experiences which are not all comfortable, and over which he has little or no control. Others will make decisions for their own good, which will affect him badly, causing pain, sorrow and hardship during his whole life. He will not understand why this is happening, but will just note that it *is* happening, and that the results for him are not very desirable.

Of course, he will still make decisions which affect others badly, and these will increase the energy field which is binding his mental and emotional bodies closely together, so that when he reaches the end of this life he will still have a large amount of un-neutralised energy to be dealt with in a future life – but at least a *small* amount of the energy field which he did have before coming into his current life will have been neutralised. However the net balance sheet of additional energy binding him will almost certainly be greater by the end of his life.

And so the process will continue, for hundreds of lives, until at last a turning point is reached, and the process can start to be reversed. Now the fact that there is a turning point at all is a very interesting phenomenon. You will remember that the original energy particles which chose the experience of becoming a complete human being were *pure energy*, and could only be joined to the mental, emotional and physical bodies by a series of interfaces, each one becoming progressively denser. It is this pure energy which provides the life force which exists in all life-forms on your planet.

Now this life force flows automatically through all your different bodies until it reaches your physical body and animates it. When that life force stops flowing, your physical body dies. But the initial intensity of the life force and the intensity of the power that eventually arrives in the physical body are dramatically different, as the life force has to flow through material of increasing density – the various subtle bodies and their interfaces – until it reaches the physical body. A good analogy would be that of water flowing down a stream and encountering more and more muddy conditions, until finally the mud is so thick that the water can only ooze through the last layer very slowly. Another analogy would be the flow of electrical current through a bank of resistors, each of which cuts down the power which is delivered at the end point.

But to continue our water analogy, provided that the initial force of water remains constant – and provided there is no more mud added – sooner or later it will wash away more and more of the mud, starting with that which is nearest and least dense, thereby delivering more water at the final point. Now exactly the same thing occurs within the human condition: the life force is initially unable to do more than trickle through the physical human being, but as many hundreds of lives pass, during which time it is in continual contact with the mental body, eventually it starts to affect that mental body and to help it to see a connection between what directed thoughts the human being has and the resulting effects in the life.

This is then the turning point, beyond which Numan starts to use his mental faculties more logically, and certainly more positively, in order to improve his own quality of life. Of course, he cannot avoid the effects of all those things that he has already done, but at least he can stop adding to the burden which he has incurred, and can start to reduce the backlog of unresolved energy which remains to be neutralised.

*   *   *

But we do not intend to give you the impression that everything changes overnight. By the time that the turning point is reached, Numan has already lived many hundreds of lives during which he has amassed a great deal of unresolved energy – which we can rightly describe as negative energy, as it is having the effect of stopping him from completing his journey through the final stage on Earth and going on to explore other planets within your solar system. All the negative energy which has been amassed must be neutralised, and as there will probably be many more hundreds of lives which must be lived in order for him to achieve release, the journey will not be easy for him.

But the overall number of lives required to release all the negative energy will be only about half of the number already lived, as once the turning point has been passed, the extent of Numan's knowledge and understanding increases at an accelerating pace, as more and more of the mud which stopped the primary life force flowing through the mental body is washed away. This means that the emotional body also starts to be affected, as the mental and emotional bodies are closely linked.

At this stage an interesting phenomenon occurs. Numan begins to notice that there is a link between the emotional body and the physical body, and to realise that when the former is badly affected it will have a resultant effect on the latter. Not immediately, of course, as in your world things happen painfully slowly, viewed from our perspective. But over a period of time there are certainly changes in the physical body which are caused to some extent by the emotions which have been experienced.

Once more, this realisation does not come about overnight, but over the period of many lives, during which there is a gradual enlightenment about how the body works, how the different bodies are interlinked – after having first reached an understanding that there *are* different bodies – and how this knowledge can be used to modify behaviour in the current life in order to create an easier and a more successful existence, with less danger of creating more negative energy for future lives.

There is another turning point later, although this is more of a dramatic change in speed rather than a change in direction, and this comes when enough of the mud has been washed away from the mental body to allow Numan to start to see the whole process of life, and to understand it. Up to this time, there has never been any recollection of past lives: the mental processes have been so limited that Numan has thought that the current life was the only one he has ever had, and that there would be no other one to follow. But at a certain time he begins to get a glimpse of the true reality, and may in fact have experiences, either in dream-state or in momentary waking flashbacks, of previous existences.

At this point he may also start to have what you call psychic experiences, or be in a group of people who themselves are having similar experiences. In fact, it is at this point in time when the Law of Attraction starts to show itself in a positive way. The Law of Attraction states that things which are of the same basic nature will be attracted to each other. You have a visible example of this in the Law of Gravity, which is the force which holds you all on the planet, and stops you floating off into outer space. You also have the phrase "Birds of a feather flock together," which describes not only the situation in the animal world but also the human situation.

8. Energy Fields and the Chakra System

Some of you are aware that surrounding the physical human body there is a force field, which you call the *Aura*. This force field is composed of the energy fields of the different bodies – mental, emotional and physical – complete with their respective interfaces, which have been engineered to allow the basic entity to operate as a human being. The energy field of the physical body is relatively small, extending out beyond the body for only one or two inches, but the fields of the other bodies extend out much further – in certain cases to several feet from the physical body. Now if you come into the company of someone who is of a similar nature to yourself – you would say *compatible* with you – there will be a positive interaction between your two auras which will be comfortable, and each of you will experience a certain warmth of feeling.

But if you come into the energy field of someone who is not compatible with you, you will both experience a negative interaction, and both of you will feel uneasy, and this unease will be neutralised only when you move away from each other. The net result of that fact is that you will tend to be drawn to – and actively seek out – the company of those who are compatible with you, and shy away from those whose auras make you feel uncomfortable.

When you come to the second turning point in your life, you start to become considerably more sensitive to your surroundings, and one of the results of this is that you will notice the interaction of your own aura with those of other people more and more, so that – given a choice – you will actively steer clear of those who are *not on your wavelength*. Or perhaps you will say that you get *bad vibes* from those people, as opposed to the *good vibes* which you get from those with whom you would want to associate.

Once Numan gets to this stage in his journey on your Earth he has reached the state where he can start to actively take control of his life, and ensure that he is working with the forces which will create harmonious conditions in all his dealings with other human beings.

* * *

At this point the process of neutralisation of the negative energy which has built up over so many lives speeds up dramatically, as there will be little more negativity created in the successive lives of Numan, who is now fully aware of what has held him tied to your planet for so many hundreds of lives. Even the most enlightened of beings can have moments of weakness, so we hesitate to say that there will be *no* more negativity, but in general terms each successive life will succeed in making a large reduction in the overall amount of negativity, until eventually the point is reached where there is nothing more to neutralise, and Numan can at last be free.

So when he dies for the final time, not only does the physical body disintegrate, closely followed by the lowest level of interface, but also the emotional body, which has no further purpose, and its own interface. But something strange now occurs: the mental body, which has been working closely through its own interface with the primary source of energy, has become by now – over many hundreds of lives – so infused with the primary energy that it has taken on a character of its own. The primary source of energy, which has been up to now unfocused, has found out that it can be more effective when channelled through the mental body, and so it remains together with that mental body and its interface as a separate entity, and can project itself as it once did when it was associated with a physical body.

A simple analogy here would be that the sun's rays may be relatively mild when shining on the skin of a human being, but when focussed through a lens would very soon create an intolerable sensation of burning.

When Numan reaches this level of development, he is free of all ties to the Earth, and able to travel at will throughout the galaxy, although on occasions, like many others who have reached the same level, he will choose to remain close to the Earth in order to help other human beings in their journey through the many lives which stretch before them. But the fact that Numan is free of the bonds of Earth does not mean that he has finished his journey, for he has many other adventures before him. He will experience existences on other planets within the solar system and travelling through different dimensions. Then finally, in a future time unimaginably remote from your own, his mental body and its own interface finally disintegrate and all the particles of which they are composed are absorbed into the totality of energy from which everything began in the first place. At that moment, the end of a great cycle will have come, and everything will be ready to return to the original primeval state of being, as it was before the Big Bang.

* * *

Author's Note: *In a very neat and simple way the story of Numan solves the age-old enigma of Free Will v. Predestination, without mentioning either word specifically. For the first few hundred years Numan has total Free Will, but in each of his actions he is building up Karmic debts which will have to be neutralised – and is in fact creating his own Predestination for future lives!*

The channelling continues:

The most significant fact to emerge from all of this is:

1. the mental body is the most durable

2. of all the bodies of a human being

3. and will last until the very end of Time itself

4. until just before the next Big Bang.

This mental body will remain as a constant long after the human being has ended his or her life on your planet. Indeed, in our dimension, which is one in which mind and pure energy are almost seamlessly joined together, we still have a mental body, and this mental body enables us to contact human beings and, in some cases, reveal to them who we were during our last journey on your Earth.

So the mental body is eternal, and is closely allied to the primary energy which is the source of all manifestation. So what does that mean to you as an individual? Well, putting it as simply as we can, in one word –

Everything!

1. That mental body is part of your present makeup,

2. is part of your very being,

3. and it has access to unlimited energy.

Could anything be more important, or more exciting, than that?

Of course that mental body is working through an emotional body, a physical body, and their respective interfaces in order to take part in the experiences which you have in your everyday life, so it is not surprising that you do not realise what you are, or how powerful you are. You think that you are subject to the whims and caprices of fortune, and have little or no influence over your own destiny. Well, you have probably heard of the saying "As you think, so you are," and this is certainly true, did you but know it. If you think that you are a loser, that is what you most certainly *will* be, whereas if you think that everything will turn out for the best, you will have far more chance of success.

Let us try to explain how all this works. First, we must say that thought is one of the strongest forces in the universe – and the reason is quite simply that thought is an energy – the closest thing to the primary energy of which we have spoken. Everything that you ever do starts off as a thought. Remember that the power of thought is what distinguishes human beings from animals. When you are acting on a purely instinctive level, you are acting as an animal does. In saying this we are not deriding the force of instinct, as it is very important still in human behaviour: for instance, without the instinct for self-preservation or the mating instinct your race would have died out many millennia ago. But we are talking about you as a human being, and of your capacity to rise above the level of animal behaviour.

When we talk about thought, we have to realise that thoughts range from fleeting impressions, or daydreams, through simple planning exercises – deciding what you are going to eat, or where you are going to go – up to wrestling with the most abstruse mental problems posed by Mathematics or Philosophy – and each of these thoughts have some influence on the world around you. How can this be? Well, in order to understand it we really have to go a long way back in our explanations, to the psychic constitution of the human body and tell you of the influences which affect how it works.

* * *

We stated that a group of particles which had come to the end of their experiences as atoms in parts of a human body had the impulse which made them gather round them a mental and an emotional body, complete with their two interfaces, before being ready to enter a foetus which was already in the mother's womb. We said that while in that foetus they created the last interface which would allow the final attachment to the physical body as the new human being. So all of the bodies – and their interfaces – were formed out of the particles which are the primary energy of the whole of created form, and which may truly be seen as Life itself – eternal Life.

Now the physical body of the human being can receive life only from life which already exists – it cannot create life by itself. So, while it is still in the womb and attached to the mother, it does not have any existence separate from the mother. Once it has been born, it can no longer receive the life force from the mother, and has to rely on its own ability to receive the universal life force from the particles which *are* life – the particles of primary energy. But in order to do that it has to have organs which will allow the transmission of this force to take place.

Fortunately, there are in each created life-form exactly such organs, without which no life could exist at all. We need not trouble ourselves with the mechanisms which exist in life-forms at other levels on your planet, as we are concerned only with what affects human beings. So we will go on now to specify exactly what those mechanisms are.

Within each human being there are a number of psychic receptors which are able to receive information from external sources. The most important of these receptors are those which are able to receive the primal life force, which exists everywhere in the universe, and to transmit it to the physical body to allow that body to function. There are seven major receptors, although many more minor ones, and these major receptors are so arranged that they form a line from one end of the spine to the other. Those who have the gift of being able to see energy perceive these receptors as spinning wheels of light, and since in one of the most ancient of your sacred languages the word for *wheel* is *chakra*, that is the name which has become associated with these receptors, and is the name which we will use.

We have explained how the human being was originally formed, and it was at this remote time in the past that the original receptors were built into each of the bodies in turn. There are no organs within the physical body which are directly linked to the chakras, although there are the vestiges of one primeval organ which was once used in connection with receiving external information. Let us briefly outline the positions of the chakras and their functions.

The first three chakras are the ones which are closely associated with the physical body, and are as follows:

The Base Chakra. Situated at the base of the spine, it is associated with the grounding of the person into a physical, third-dimensional existence.

The Sacral Chakra, just below the navel, is connected with the sexual functions, and the organs in that part of the body.

The Solar Plexus Chakra is just below the rib-cage. It connects closely to the emotions, and also with the force of Will.

The Heart Chakra is the gateway to the non-physical bodies, and is particularly associated with non-sexual Love and Compassion.

The non-physical bodies are served by the last three chakras:

The Throat Chakra is associated with communication of all kinds.

The Third Eye Chakra, in the middle of the forehead, is connected with the psychic ability to see – or more correctly to *sense* – non-physical objects and conditions. It is the only chakra directly connected with a part of the body – the pineal gland – and in Tibetan Buddhism an operation used to be done on the pineal gland in order to promote clairvoyance in young monks.

The Crown Chakra, at the top of the head, is traditionally associated with psychic inspiration and illumination.

Now when the life force is received it has to pass through all the different bodies and their interfaces before it can finally reach the physical body, and due to the increasing density through which it has to pass, only a relatively small amount of force is finally able to be used.

* * *

So is there any other factor which affects the amount of life force which is received by any one of you? There are other factors, although none are so important as the condition of the major receptors. One of these factors is the kind of food that is eaten by the individual. You know that you need food in order to survive, and – particularly in your modern age when so much emphasis is being placed on the physical body and its shape – you are well aware of proteins, fats, carbohydrates, minerals and vitamins. But what you are not so aware of is the importance of the *kind* of food, and how it has been treated before it arrives on your plate.

Remember once more that everything that you eat is comprised of primary particles of energy, which have an increasing level of organisational complexity as they move up the different levels of life-forms – the greater the degree of complexity, the greater the density of the organism. Since the life force *is* the energy within those particles, the more complexity that there is, and the more density, then the less of that life force will be able to be received. That means that if you can make a substantial proportion of your daily intake of food plant material – particularly *raw* plants – then you will be able to receive a greater proportion of benefit from the vital energy within those plants.

As you increase your intake of processed plant food, you are adding more and more complexity and so are deriving less and less benefit from your diet, *regardless of the nutritional value of what you are eating.* As far as diet is concerned, you are already becoming aware of the dangers to your physical health of so many of the additives of all sorts which are put into your food for various reasons, but so far you are almost totally oblivious to the harm that is being done in reducing the life force within whatever you are eating.

When we talk about processed food, there is a certain amount of processing which you do in your own home, regardless of what you buy. Cooking itself is one thing which reduces the amount of life force available in food, although it is essential in preparing certain foods to make them digestible. Many traditional ways of cooking use long periods of preparation and slow cooking, which are less destructive, but in your modern world, with so many quick and easy ways of cooking, such as infra-red devices or – particularly – microwave devices, you run the risk of totally removing any life force which may still exist in the food. You cannot destroy that life force, since energy is indestructible, but what you actually do is block the possibility of you assimilating it while you are eating the food.

* * *

So far, we have mentioned only the processing of food derived from plants. How about food from animal sources? Well, here there are two separate considerations: the first is that in introducing another level of food – animals – you are increasing the complexity of the organism, which we have pointed out is not a good thing to do, as it decreases the amount of life force which is eventually available at the level of the physical body. But the second consideration is more important: the conditions in which the animals are raised before being eventually slaughtered must be taken into account. When animals are living in a normal healthy environment in the wild, and killed quickly, there is little reduction in the life force. But as soon as you keep animals in unnatural conditions, particularly in what you call factory farms, then there is a considerable deterioration.

Remember that we are speaking only of the amount of life force available within various kinds of foods, *not* about their intrinsic value as nourishment for the physical body. You already have so many books about the latter that it would be of little value to repeat what you already know.

So are there other ways of receiving the life force? Once again the answer is, "Yes!" and one of these ways is from other human beings. We have said that there are many receptors within the human body which are capable of receiving information – and we have deliberately kept that term vague in order to cover a variety of things which can be received. But considering specifically the life force, there are many minor chakras which are involved in its absorption, through interchange between human beings. Two of the most important of these minor chakras are the nipples on the breasts, through which a mother would naturally feed her child for the first few months of its life. Through these nipples the baby receives not only nourishment, but also some of the mother's life force – and it is this fact which reinforces the bonding between the mother and the child.

Of course, in your modern enlightened age there has been a movement away from mothers breast-feeding their children, and giving them processed foods instead. Think of the damage you are doing in interfering with the processes of Nature which have served your race for many millennia: introducing artificial instead of natural processes increases complexity, and so reduces the amount of life force which the baby receives. But more serious is the fact that strong bonds between mother and children are the basis for family unity, and any weakening of those bonds can obviously have grave repercussions in later life.

There are also minor chakras in the palms of the hands, and when a baby is small, it is continually handled by the mother or by other relatives, which once again increases the bonding as well as giving the baby the extra life force it needs.

Another way in which the life force is received by all human beings is from the sun. You are aware of its life-giving energy as light and heat, without which you could not exist. You know that it is important in the absorption of one of your vitamins into the body, and you also know that some people are very adversely affected during the times of the year when there is little sunlight. But the sun's rays have a far wider importance in your life.

Throughout history, recorded or not, there have been whole civilisations which have realised the importance of the sun, and some have even worshipped it as a god. Perhaps the next time that you are sun-bathing, and enjoying the warmth of the physical rays, you may also think of the spiritual aspect, and consciously breathe in the very life force of the universe at the same time.

Some of you are already well aware that the strongest emanation of this life force is not when the sun is at its highest, and so hottest: it is when the sun first appears over the morning horizon. Those of you who have had the experience of seeing the sunrise will already know what a truly magical time it is.

The final way in which life force is received is through the power of thought, either from others or by their own action, so this is the point at which we can return to what we were saying about the power of thought.

We have explained how you are surrounded by a veritable sea of particles. That is a very good way for you to understand what and where you are – an island of solid matter in an ocean of pure energy. This energy is the energy of Creation itself, as out of it has come everything which you can accept as created matter, so this energy is the energy of the *potential*.

Some of the more inspired of your scientists have already become aware of this, and yet even they have only scratched the surface of the true reality, as they have not yet made the connection between the potential energy of the universe and the power of the human mind. So let us add a little more information on the matter.

First, let us look at the human mind – what we term the human mental body – as a passive organ of receptivity. Throughout history, and particularly the recorded history of science, there have been examples of people who have had a sudden idea of how to explain why things happen as they do. Sometimes these ideas have come in the form of dreams, at other times they have come as a result of observing a physical occurrence – Newton's apple falling from a tree, Fleming's mould growing on a Petri dish or Archimedes' bathtub. But however the ideas have occurred, they have started a train of research which has led to great advances in knowledge.

What has happened is that those people have been able for a moment to tune into the primary energy field and see the potential explanation of the phenomenon in question. They have then – by the application of concentrated thought – been able to turn this into a working hypothesis, and finally into a provable law. The common word which you use for all these events is *inspiration*, which is actually very true, as in its purest form that word means *breathing in*. In each of the cases, and in countless others, the person has been literally able to breathe in the knowledge and recognise a part of the overall potential of the universe made manifest on the Earth.

So there are a large number of chakras which have an effect on the human body, and many of these have the function of receiving information from external sources. Most human beings have had experiences at one time or other in their lives where they have been given information which they could not have received by conventional means. This is often described as intuition, and a wide variety of experiences are lumped together under the same heading.

Stories abound of people who have refused to take a planned flight in an aeroplane which later crashed, or to catch a train which later had an accident. Even the greatest of your scientists have never been able to explain such phenomena adequately, and yet the truth is simple. Those who were involved have been able – subconsciously – to tune into the primary energy field, have noted the potential events in that field, and have taken conscious decisions which have saved their lives.

Some individuals, of course, will always be better at doing certain things than others, and as some people have this ability already developed to a high degree when they are born, you coin a word for them: you call them *psychics*. Many people from childhood are able to "hear voices" or to "see" non-physical beings. Others deliberately choose to develop these abilities through a variety of physical or mental disciplines. All humans are capable of using far more of their innate powers, and as you come to recognise more of the truth about yourselves and your own potential, there will be an increasing number of you who will seek to use these powers which are latent within you.

A variation of the ability to use the psychic receptors is that of receiving signals from other parts of the solar system, galaxy or the universe as a whole. This is a fairly rare form of psychic ability: it is rare because there are few people who can accept that there *are* other beings apart from themselves within the universe, and that disbelief effectively prevents all possibility of communication.

But the normal way in which psychics use their abilities is to receive contact from others who have left physical existence, but who still continue to exist in a non-physical dimension until a further re-birth at a later time. Since a large proportion of the previous life on Earth has been taken up with emotional experiences gained through contact with other human beings, it is not surprising that there will usually be a desire on the part of the *dear departed* to contact those still on Earth to reassure them about the fact that they still exist.

Such discarnate beings can still make contact with the grieving loved ones, but with great difficulty. Their ability to do so will depend on several factors:

1. how sensitive the loved ones are – i.e. how well developed their psychic receptors are;

2. how much they realise that there *is* a continued existence after the death of the physical body;

3. to what extent have they been "brain-washed" by others – usually religious organisations – about the evils of contacting the dead;

4. the fear of actually being *able* to make contact.

But even in the best of conditions, the dear departed themselves have first to reach the stage of understanding at which *they* are able to communicate. If they themselves believe that communication is not possible, then they will not even try. With so many obstacles to overcome from both sides it is not surprising that they make contact with great difficulty.

But whatever the difficulty, in many cases there is such love for those left behind that they continually try to communicate, and often eventually succeed. Some learn how to infiltrate into the dreams of the loved ones, and some are able to concentrate their love around their loved ones to the extent of making them aware of their presence.

Others achieve the ability to move physical objects in order to draw the attention of the loved ones to the fact that something unusual is happening. But the majority are only able to contact the loved ones by using the services of a psychic medium such as a clairvoyant or clairaudient. Interestingly enough, in many of the latter cases the loved ones themselves become so interested in the whole subject of contact that they start to make attempts develop their own psychic skills.

9. Thought and Karma

We have thoroughly covered the basic idea that you are surrounded by particles of primary energy, intelligent energy, which you can – and do – access by using your psychic receptors. These receptors receive information of various kinds, ranging from the very life force which continually energises you and enables you to exist in a physical world, to communications from discarnate entities. The interaction of the auras of two human beings when they came into close proximity to each other is also sensed through the psychic receptors.

So far, we have considered the mind as a passive organ, capable of receiving information only, but now we must go further, and consider how it can be used actively. Remember that the mental body is the nearest of the bodies of a human being to the primary energy source, and so it has the greatest ability to affect – and be affected by – that source. As that primary energy contains all the possibilities of Creation, affecting it in any way would affect the potential of what could happen, and so could affect the eventual outcome of a chain of events.

We shall take a theoretical example: just imagine that two people who are highly compatible have the potential of being in a certain area, and of passing a certain point, within minutes of each other. Just imagine that you know that this is likely, and you wish them to meet. If, by an exercise of concentrated thought, you were able to slow one of them down and/or speed up the other, you would be able to make them arrive at that point at the same time, and even to bump into each other – and leave the rest to their own psychic receptors. Fanciful? Of course it is – but not as fanciful as you may think. Because *thought uses energy*, and by concentrating this energy you can *change Reality*.

Let us explain this further: first, the fact that thought uses energy. Every organ in your body needs energy in order to work, and in most cases the energy comes from a physical reaction between the chemicals in your food and the air which you breathe. The heart is different, as it uses energy which is akin to electrical energy to provide the stimulus needed to make it beat regularly many thousands of times a day. Where does that energy come from? And where does the energy which gives the brain the power to make decisions and to control so many of your bodily movements come from?

We put forward an idea which may possibly start a train of thought, and lead to further advances in understanding. What if the mental body is able to contact the primary energy field directly, and draw from it the energy to power its own activities? And what if the physical organ which is the heart also has its own *mental body* which is able to do the same thing?

* * *

We shall leave that last consideration to your medical researchers, for we wish to develop the first theme and see if it can possibly explain what can – and does – happen in your world.

When you think of the possibility of something happening, the energy for that thought comes from your mental body, which receives its power from the primary energy force. As this force also contains the potential of everything which could possibly happen, a field of possibility within that force is created. As the primary energy force contains *all* possibilities, including the *probability* of what *will* happen eventually, whatever you have thought of *reinforces* the existing possibility of that thing happening. Whether or not a single thought will have any influence on the probability depends on what others factors are combining together to create that probability: in most cases it will not. But if the initial thought is not *casual* – "I *wonder* whether XYZ will happen" – but *directed* – "I *intend* XYZ to happen" – then the effect is far more powerful.

It may help if you imagine all the possible outcomes of a particular situation being put up on a ladder, almost like a league table. The one with the highest possibility goes at the top of the ladder, where it has the title of *probability*, while the others are ranked below it in order of their respective likelihood.

Do you see what is likely to happen if that same thought is expressed over and over again? The possibility of the thing happening is continually increased, and so moves up the ladder, until eventually the new possibility *becomes greater than* the probability which already exists – and so replaces it.

This is such a fundamental factor in your human lives that its importance cannot be over-emphasised. You are continually creating your own future by the thoughts which you express in your everyday life – and nowhere is this more evident than in the thoughts which you have about yourself.

Let us consider the early lives of two fictional children, who lived in similar environments and family circumstances: one of the children – whom we shall call Tom – was told from a very early age that he was naughty or bad, stupid or useless, ugly or clumsy, and those ideas percolated into his young consciousness until eventually he came to believe that they were true.

By contrast, the other boy – Harry – was continually praised, and told how good, clever, intelligent, skilful or handsome he was, so these ideas sank into his consciousness and conditioned *him* to believe that they were facts.
Which boy do you think was more likely to live a happy and productive life? Of course it was Harry. Whatever the earlier

conditioning had been for either child, that mindset was taken by him into the primary school, where he acted out the role of the character which he thought that he was. And the child's teachers were likely to react to that role-play, which merely served to reinforce the self-image that the child already had. The same scenario would be enacted in secondary school, so that by the time the child reached adulthood he had *become* that person.

Once adulthood is reached, it is very unlikely that the basic character will ever be changed during whatever remains of the life, without some dramatic intervention from some external source – such as a psychologist, counsellor or religious advisor – who will be able to explain what has happened and how the whole of the previous conditioning can be reversed. So where the early conditioning has been negative, the rest of the life of that person is likely to be spent in quite unpleasant circumstances.

In Tom's case, this was nowhere more evident that in his experiences in relationships. Throughout his teenage years he had few friends, and even fewer girl-friends, and those relationships which he formed usually fizzled out fairly rapidly. As an adult, the same pattern was to repeat itself: the only girls with whom he seemed to be able to have any sort of relationship at all were those who, like him, were life's losers – and in those cases it seemed that the only thing which bound the couple together for any length of time was the fear of being left alone outside the relationship. So Tom had a string of failed relationships, and eventually sought temporary oblivion in drink and drugs, and trudged through his adult life in an atmosphere of dejection and self-deprecation.

We have mentioned the phrase *external source* and sometimes the external source might be something dramatic like a serious accident, or a life-threatening incident or illness, which forces the person to review his life to date and ask why it developed as it did. But should this happen, he is still likely to seek advice from some other individual, professional or amateur. If he goes through a series of counselling sessions, he may begin to understand what has been happening.

So what would create the conditions in which the lives of the two boys become so different? Here, we have to go back to what was said when we were discussing Astrology. The influences of the various astrological bodies at the moment of birth decided whether the initial parenting was of poor quality, as in Tom's case, or favourable, as in Harry's. But ultimately, the cause was the state of the energy which surrounded the spiritual entity before it chose to enter into the foetus. In many Eastern religious traditions there is the idea that you will get back whatever you have given out in the past, and this is called *Karma*. We have already explained that the workings of this principle are connected with the fact that the negative energy from many acts over many lives has formed a coating round the human subtle bodies which stops the mental and emotional bodies from disintegrating on the death of the physical body. So as it is far easier to use the one word, *Karma*, than the words *surrounding negative energy field*, that is what we will use in future.

In Tom's case some of the existing Karma which has accumulated round his mental and emotional bodies may have been neutralised by the end of his life, although he might also incur fresh Karma by his actions during that life. What about Harry? Well, he certainly didn't have many of the problems which Tom encountered, but that doesn't mean that he had a charmed life. Some problems might occur which would allow him to neutralise part of his own Karma, but how he reacted to these situations would decide whether he ended it with more or less Karma than he started with.

We hope that a broad picture is now beginning to emerge, the picture of initial particles of energy banding together and creating bodies and interfaces which enable them to have the experience of living in a human body. But after the initial experience of life as a human being, the different bodies are no longer able to disintegrate because the Karma, which has been generated by their actions during that life, continues to bind them together. So they are forced to remain together as a single entity, after the death and disintegration of the physical body, until all of the Karma which surrounds them and binds them together has been neutralised and dispersed. This is done when each individual experiences the same conditions as those which the entity has caused to others in a previous life or lives. And the mechanism which determines what conditions are likely to be experienced in any one life is that of the solar and galactic influences which are prevalent on the Earth at the moment of birth.

Author's Note: *The term "entity" would in certain religions be known as "the soul," but at this stage those channelling preferred to use the word "entity."*

* * *

Let us return to our consideration of what we may rightly call *the power of thought*. We have explained how *directed* thought – or if you prefer it, *concentrated* thought – can be used to bring about a desired situation. You call this *manifestation*. So let us return to the example of the two boys, Tom and Harry. We started by saying that from an early age Tom was told that he was bad and stupid. Who would have told him that? In most cases it would have been his own parents, but it could well have been a number of other people, including grandparents, brothers, sisters, uncles, aunts, cousins, neighbours, teachers, or even strangers.

It doesn't really matter who said these things – the important thing for Tom was that they *were* said, and we have seen the disastrous effect that they had on the whole of his later life. It is rightly said that the influences experienced in a child's first few years will condition him for the rest of his life. But now let us consider the matter from the point of view of those who actually *said* them: they did something which eventually harmed someone else, and by doing so *they* incurred Karma. According to the primary Law of which we have spoken earlier – the law of Cause and Effect – that Karma had to be dealt with, and that would mean that they will experience exactly the same situation in their own life.

Now if they are already an adult, it may not be possible for them to have this experience during that same life, so the negative energy which they have created will be added to their overall Karma and will have to be dealt with later. This is why, in some traditions, Karma is explained as the Law of Retribution and Reward, but a better term might be the phrase, "What goes around, comes around." Whatever you do to others will inevitably come back to you: there is no escaping it – you have created a condition, a negative energy, which sooner or later will be returned to you.

As a simple example of this, suppose that you have derided and mocked someone who has a physical or mental disability – perhaps someone was physically ugly – and you took every opportunity to remind them of the fact. What would be a suitable way to learn that such conduct is not acceptable? By the simple expedient of being born with the same – or a similar – disability yourself in a future life, and spending the whole of that lifetime having to cope with all the prejudice that it caused.

Author's Note: *Obviously this is not the only reason for people to be born with physical or mental handicaps. There are many different reasons for this, and they will be covered at a later point in the book.*

The channelling session continues:

But people can harm others in many different ways – so far we have discussed only conditioning them to believe that they are inferior. Of course, a far more straightforward way of harming others is to cause them physical injury. Here again, of course, we have another application of the overall law of Cause and Effect – whatever you do to someone else, you will have done to you.

In one of your religious books you have the phrase "An eye for an eye and a tooth for a tooth." What could be more explicit? If you blind someone, you will be blinded at some time or other, in that life or in a future one. Incidentally, that verse has been taken by many people as a licence to retaliate and immediately do the same thing to whoever has done it to you. Not so – in fact exactly the reverse – as if you retaliate you will incur Karma for harming the person, so that in the future exactly the same will be done to you *again*. So why have you suffered it in the first place? Possibly because in a previous life you caused blindness to someone else, and now the wheel has come full circle: you have reaped what you have earlier sown.

In the cases like these, there are many who believe that Karma will ensure that it is *you* who will blind the other person in a future life. Once again, not so! For if this were true, it would lock the two of you together in an endless tit-for-tat retaliation until the end of time. The person who blinded you has incurred the Karma of being blinded. You have neutralised your own Karma for what you did, and can now move on – the two things are completely separate. There are some who believe that when you meet that other person in a future life and get the opportunity to blind him, you will achieve great reward for not doing so. We would prefer to say that you merely show how much you have moved on in your own development by refusing to take that opportunity.

But the full application of the law of Cause and Effect can cause apparent anomalies, where the final effects appear to be much greater than the initial cause. Consider, for instance the case of a person who kills another in one life, and who may well be paying off the Karma caused by his action for many future lives. How can this be so?

If we examine the extreme case of one man murdering another, he is affecting not only that one man, but everyone who knew and loved, cared for or respected him. That man was someone's son, and may well have been a brother, husband, or father to other people. He would probably have had friends, and may well have had workmates or colleagues. There could have been others whom he was helping in some capacity, official or personal, and so on. His sudden death would probably have affected and harmed a great number of people, so the Karma which the murderer would have incurred by that one act would be far greater than could be neutralised by his own death at the hands of another. He would have to neutralise all the other Karma which he had incurred in harming all those other people as well – *by having the same things done to him.*

And are there other ways we can harm others, which fall short of physical injury or mental conditioning? Yes, there are, but not in a form that most human beings would even think possible. For, once again, thoughts are energy, and whatever we think about others will have some sort of effect on them, whether or not that effect can ever be measured.

At one end of the scale, we can think harmful thoughts and *express those thoughts to other people*. In this case, we have harmed the objects of our displeasure by poisoning the minds of others about them, which could well have an effect of turning those others against them, and negatively influencing their future interactions. This is very often found among young people, where cliques form and share a common dislike of anyone outside the immediate circle. Such cliques are frequently the source of bullying in schools, which can range from physical abuse to mental and emotional torture. Later on in life, such cliques may become gangs, and you are now seeing the social consequences of teenage gangs roaming your streets.

More difficult to understand is the situation regarding negative thoughts about others which are never expressed, but kept privately within the mind of the individual. Can such thoughts really be harmful to them? Once again, the answer must be, "Yes!" Those thoughts still use energy, and when they are expressed they will direct that negative energy at the other person, and it will merge with the energy which makes up his/ her overall energy field and affect it slightly. A single thought might not be too harmful, but the same thought expressed many times over a period of time could well have a general depressing affect on the individual who is the target. But no matter what eventual effect it has, the same law of Cause and Effect will still apply, and what you give out you will receive back.

* * *

But what happens when you have a negative effect on someone else without consciously wishing to do so? Do you incur Karma in such a case or not? The answer is very simple – No! Karma is concerned with the energy field which you build up round yourselves as a result of your *deliberate* thoughts or actions. So let us consider how you might affect others involuntarily:

Let us refer to our classic case of Tom and Harry – a most useful example that we will refer to from time to time.

Tom has had a dismal life, shunned and despised as a child, bullied as a teenager, a loser as an adult, and so he has built up a wall of negativity round himself. He believes that he is useless, that he will never have any luck in life, that he can expect only difficulties and hardship and that everyone and everything – including God if he believes in such a being – will always be against him. We have said that thoughts are energy, and so his thoughts have been continually creating negative energy throughout his life. Now he is totally surrounded by it, and it creates a wall of negativity which blocks out any possibility of positive things happening to him.

So what is going to happen when Tom comes into the company of anyone else? All human beings have their own force field, which is composed of the energy in their different subtle bodies. Although this force field is not visible to most human beings, certain advanced psychics are able to see it as a radiant glow around the whole body. The usual word for this field is the *aura*.

Although most human beings are unable to see the auras of others, that does not mean that they are totally oblivious to them. When they come into the company of another person, that person's aura – which may stretch out for several feet from the physical body – will impinge upon their own aura, beginning an *exchange of energy* between the two. In a similar way, when a painter using water-colours puts two blobs of paint near each other on a wet surface, they may each starts to spread out towards each other.

Let us imagine that we have a man called Peter who meets Tom. Peter is an ordinary human being, without any particularly developed psychic knowledge or skills, so he does not know anything at all about auras, and certainly does not feel anything happening in his own. He is Mr Average, and has an aura which is relatively neutral, being neither decidedly positive nor decidedly negative. But after a time in Tom's company, he starts feeling ill at ease, and by the time he eventually leaves him, he feels thoroughly depressed. What has happened? A partial exchange of energy has taken place, so that some of Tom's negative energy has entered Peter's aura, and has affected him negatively. By contrast, some of Peter's aura, which is considerably more positive, has entered Tom's aura, so that *he* now feels slightly *better* than when they first met.

Although he has no specific understanding about what has happened, Peter is not a fool, and when he has been in Tom's company several times and realises that he feels depressed every time, he starts to put two and two together and comes to the conclusion that Tom is not a good person to be around. So he either shuns his company completely or he makes sure that any chance meetings are over as quickly as possible. And what effect does that have on Tom? It just reinforces his own lack of self-esteem – no one likes his company.

What happened between Tom and Peter is something that happens to all human beings: they come into the company of others, and there is a continual exchange of energy taking place. In some cases the auras of the two persons concerned are at about the same levels of positivity/negativity, but in most cases there will be a difference – and that difference will have an effect on both parties.

There are certain conditions where there is bound to be a lot of negative energy about: there is not too much laughter, for instance, at a funeral, or round the hospital bed of a terminally-ill patient. So if you are aware of what we have said about auras and exchanges of energy, what can you do to protect yourself when entering these conditions. The easiest thing to do is to imagine putting your whole aura inside a bubble of light, a sort of balloon which will reflect away all negative energy coming from any auras which you may touch while you are in that situation. If you do this as a conscious thought you will be surprised at how unaffected you may be by whatever is going on round you.

So let us sum up briefly:

1. Thoughts are energy, and your thoughts can affect others.

2. Directed, deliberate thoughts, particularly over a period of time, can affect others more greatly than random thoughts – but *all* have some effect, however small. Eventually, by the law of Cause and Effect, all will have to be either paid for, or – in the case of positive thoughts – the person sending them out will benefit from them.

3. The thoughts that you have *about yourselves* can be particularly devastating, as they could well affect not only the way that *others* see you but also the conditions which you experience in your everyday lives.

10. Thought and Health

But there is a far more serious reason why you should try to avoid negative thoughts, either about yourself or about others, and that is that such thoughts can eventually affect your own personal health, with sometimes devastating consequences. Let us examine how this could possibly happen.

Just imagine that there is something going on in your life which you can recognise, but that you don't want to accept. It may be a situation in your own family, or the character of a friend, or the fact that you yourself are behaving in a way which you know will eventually lead to unhappiness, either to you or to someone close to you. What are you doing? Well, in everyday language, you are turning a blind eye to the situation.

This does not necessarily harm you in the short term – after all, most human beings tend to avoid facing up to reality from time to time, until eventually something happens which makes them take action. But let us imagine that the situation continues for a considerable length of time, and you still refuse to accept what is happening. What you are doing is deliberately failing to accept what your eyes are seeing – and sooner or later this will start to seep from your mental body, through the interface into your emotional body, and then through that interface into your physical body. It will then start to affect your physical body *by causing problems in your eyes*. After all, you are virtually saying that your eyes are not functioning correctly when they are sending you signals about the situation, so they will eventually accept the way in which you are conditioning them *and will cease to operate so effectively*.

Let us stress that this will not happen overnight – it will take a long while for any physical results to make themselves manifest. But eventually, as long as you maintain the attitude of keeping your head in the sand, the physical effects will be experienced – and you will wonder why. The simple explanation is that it is just another example of the universal law of Cause and Effect.

If you find it hard to understand how this situation could possibly come about, let us take a simple practical example from your everyday world. Just imagine that you are going out one day for a long walk through a very heavy thunderstorm. In the morning, you had put on upper clothing of a vest, a shirt, and a pullover, and in order to go out you put on a jacket and an overcoat. Now with all those layers of clothing on there would be no possibility of your skin becoming wet.

But after you have trudged through the storm for a certain period of time, the rain will have soaked through your overcoat and will now start to wet your jacket. After a further long period, your jacket will also have become sodden, and the rain will start to wet your pullover. And then, increasingly quickly, your pullover, shirt and vest will become wet until finally you are feeling the water which has seeped through all your layers of clothing onto your skin. It will take a long time, but eventually it *will* happen.

Does that all sound very far-fetched to you? Have you dismissed as being totally impossible the idea that your thoughts can have an effect on your physical body? If so, think again, for such things *do* happen. This is all part of the problems with having a physical body, and not realising how your thoughts and emotions can affect that body.

We have mentioned the word *emotions* and perhaps you are more able to understand how your emotions can affect you physically. What do you feel, physically, if you are terrified? You feel a tightening of the muscles around your solar plexus area, and you may also feel physically sick. What do you feel when you are under great mental stress? The muscles in the back of your neck tighten up, and start to cause you headaches. What do you feel when you think that you are being imposed upon, either by some named person or persons or by life itself? Your shoulders start to ache. You even have a saying, that someone has the world on his shoulders. So if you can be physically affected by your emotions in that way, you should be able to accept at least the *possibility* that mental attitudes can also affect your physical body.

Probably the most profound of all emotions is that of falling in love: many thousands of books have been written about that and about the mental and physical effects it has on even the most down-to-earth human beings – just another example of how the mental, emotional and physical bodies are interlinked.

Once you start to explore this possibility, then you may be able to understand at least *some* of the physical conditions which affect you or others in your environment. If you have problems with hearing, are there things in your life which you don't *want* to hear? If you have problems with mobility, is there a possibility that you do not *want* to move forward in your life? Respiratory problems? Do you feel that somehow you haven't the *right* to get the most out of life? How about problems with the heart? Do you allow love and joy to flow through your heart, or are you less and less able to feel the joy of life itself?

Two of the most prevalent medical problems in your modern society concern the back and the bowels. So many people suffer with backache without knowing quite what to do about it. But the back is the main means of support of the whole body, and feeling the lack of support in your life can lead to problems with the back. If you feel the lack of emotional support, the result is likely to be felt in the upper back, while the lack of financial support is more likely to lead to lower back problems.

As far as the bowels are concerned, these are the organs of elimination of matter from the physical body. Do you have difficulty with releasing old hurts from your life, and of forgiving those who have caused them? If so, there is a strong possibility that you will have difficulties with the correct functioning of the bowels. This in itself is bad enough, but if you harbour bitterness about the past, don't be surprised if liver problems develop. Finally, long-harboured resentment can build up over the years and lead to various forms of cancer.

This is a very complex subject, and our desire is not to give you a comprehensive course in how to recognise and nullify the psychic conditions which lead to various illnesses, and tell you how to neutralise them – there are already many standard textbooks by famous psychologists and counsellors which you can consult for that. Our aim is merely to point out to you the *mechanics* of how the different non-physical bodies in the human being – often called the *subtle bodies* – react with the physical body, so that you are aware of the importance of always being in control of your thoughts and emotions – for your own sake.

Author's Note: *See Further Reading under Hay, Louise.*

The channelling continues:

****

One thing remains to be covered: why some people seem to be born *lucky* – or *unlucky*, as the case may be. How does that come about, and – more importantly – what can you do about it?

Let us start off by saying that as you live in the physical world, the majority of your experiences come about through your own interaction with other human beings, and immediately we come back to the *effect* that you have on those others. We saw the effect that Tom had on Peter: after a time Peter tried to avoid him if he could, as he realised that he always felt worse after being in his company, and we may safely presume that others might do exactly the same thing.

This would be a bad enough result for Tom if it was just a question of being ignored and left out by others in his surroundings, but it doesn't stop there. Let us imagine that Tom is employed by a small company, and his general negativity has a dampening effect on all his colleagues. Not only is he likely to be left out of their conversations, but he won't make many friends there, and if anything goes wrong he is likely to get blamed for the mistake – even if he had nothing to do with it.

Because of this, his supervisor or manager is not likely to look very kindly on him – particularly as he/she *also* feels uncomfortable in Tom's presence – so when any bonus is coming, or any easy jobs, Tom is certainly not going to be in the front line for them. But he is certainly likely to be in the front line if there are lay-offs in the company.

But how about strokes of luck? Well, let us state straight away that luck does not exist. It is just a word which has been invented by human beings to try to explain fortunate happenings by ascribing them to some nebulous external force. Luck is merely a physical demonstration of the law of Cause and Effect, which has been brought into action by the individual him/herself. To put it into plain words, *you make your own luck.*

If you go through life in an optimistic frame of mind, you are far more likely to have lucky things happen to you than if you are always pessimistic. Of course, negative things will always happen to every human being, because of the operation of Karma, but surrounding yourself with negativity is far more likely to put up a barrier to good things happening to you. Just imagine that you have the inspiration to do the lottery one week, when there is a strong possibility that your numbers will be drawn. If you say "No, I'm not going to, as I never have any luck," then you are removing any possibility of having a win – you can't win if you haven't entered.

Once more, the explanation is fairly simple: all possibilities exist, but by being totally negative and refusing to accept the possibility of anything good happening to you, you are pushing that possibility down the ladder, so that there is little chance of it ever coming into being.

So let us sum up the principles involved:

1. The mental and emotional bodies (and their interfaces) are inextricably linked with the physical body, and so have an effect on it.

2. What you feel about yourself creates an energy field around you, and that energy field can be sensed by other human beings. If you make them feel uncomfortable, they are likely to react adversely to you, with various harmful effects on your wellbeing.

3. The thoughts that you have, either about yourself or about others, are able to seep into the tissues of your physical body over a period of time, and create a wide variety of illnesses.

4. Creating a field of negativity around yourself can have the

effect of making a barrier to stop fortunate events ever occurring in your life.

5. Negative actions against, or thoughts about, another person will create a field of negative energy, which is called Karma, round your various subtle bodies which will have to be neutralised at some time in the future.

But we do not mean to imply that this Karma will necessarily have no impact until a *future* life: once the negative action or thought has taken place, the energy will *immediately* be attached to the subtle bodies, and so will start to have an effect on your aura – with all the undesirable effects which we have just described. Viewed from our perspective, the aura will become duller and more muddy in appearance, and the more additional negative thoughts and actions there are, the more the aura will be affected.

As we have already mentioned the analogy of water trying to flow down a stream, and being restricted by successive layers of mud until its flow is slowed down to a mere trickle, it is quite appropriate that we say that the colours of the aura become muddy. But the more muddy they become, the more other human beings are likely to pick up on the increasing negative energy, and progressively cut themselves off from your company. Just reading through this last paragraph will give you a very good reason for avoiding negativity completely at all times. So let us see if we can give you a few pointers how to do that.

* * *

We shall leave Tom for the time being wallowing in his far-from-ideal existence as a miserable individual with few friends and little luck, and turn our attention to Harry. He was brought up surrounded by a loving family and friends, all of whom thought that he was good, intelligent, kind and handsome. They thought this, and they also made a point of telling Harry what they thought, which meant that he grew up feeling that he was a very special boy indeed. It also meant that, surrounded by so much love, he felt very safe in his environment, and at ease with others around him.

This certainly showed itself when he went to his first school. He had been well prepared by his parents, being told how grown-up it was to go to school, and that it was a wonderful place where he would be able to learn lots of interesting things. So from the first day he felt at ease there, without too many of the little problems that children have when separated from their home environment for the first time. He quickly made many friends, and was a favourite with most of his teachers, who found him an easy pupil, with a mind eager to learn new things. Naturally he did well in his lessons, and was often given *stars* and *merit points* for his work. Success breeds success, and the praise that he received reinforced his own self-esteem and gave him even more confidence. He received praise for his achievements from both the teachers at school and from his parents and family when he came home – and all of this made him feel successful and more enthusiastic to do even better.

The pattern continued when he went to secondary school, where he quickly integrated into the larger surroundings, and rapidly gathered a large group of friends round him. He was popular with the teachers, taking a keen interest in most subjects – and tolerating those which he didn't particularly like – so that he finished school with a good scholastic record. He also found out fairly early that one of the ways of achieving respect among his fellow pupils – especially among the girls at the school – was to be good at sport, so he excelled at several sports and games. But even more importantly, he was selected as a teacher's aide and became a member of the School Council, where he made many valuable contributions in discussions concerning the smooth running of the school. As a result, by the time that he left school and went on into further education he was already a very assured, confident and level-headed young man.

The same pattern was, of course, repeated during the remainder of his career, and when he eventually applied for a job he had little trouble in sailing through his interviews, and found exactly the kind of work which he wanted. He naturally got on very well with his colleagues and was noticed by members of the management team, who earmarked him for future promotion. In his emotional life, he had so many friends – of both sexes – that he found little difficulty in getting into a stable and fulfilling relationship with someone who had a similar background, and eventually they got married and went on to raise children in the same way that they themselves had been raised.

But what about Harry's general health? Did he have any health problems during his early life? At this point we need to differentiate between the health conditions which come about because of the operation of Karma from a previous existence and those which are caused by the individual during the current life. Let us start with Karma from past lives.

Karma is the layer of energy which surrounds the mental and emotional bodies and their interfaces, and is the force which stops them from disintegrating when the person eventually dies and the physical body and its interface return to their constituent elements. At the moment we are speaking only of the negative Karma which has been accumulated during the previous succession of lives to date. And this Karma can be dispersed and neutralised by only the *opposite* conditions in the physical life of an individual, which will normally mean that the person will *receive* what they have given out or caused others to experience. But what if they have caused harm to themselves?

Let us imagine that someone has so abused their physical body during one particular lifetime that they have shown complete disregard for their own health. The possibilities of ruining one's own health are so many and varied that we will not go into many of them, but eating excessively – obesity is currently one of the greatest health problems in your Western world – drinking too much or taking recreational drugs to alter physical, mental or emotional states would certainly rank fairly high on the list. We are not being judgemental in saying this: the negative effects of such practices are already well known in your medical circles. It is also becoming realised that the taking of too many prescription drugs can also be harmful – although in most cases these are originally needed for quite legitimate medical conditions. Later on we will consider some of these topics in much greater detail.

Now if someone does abuse their bodies in the course of their life it is quite common for them to suffer for it later, as many diseases are the direct result of over-indulgence in some form or other. Heart issues due to obesity and liver problems due to over-use of alcohol are only two of the many examples we could quote. But can the actions in one life directly affect the next life of the person concerned? Once more, let us go back to first principles: deliberately disregarding your own health will create a negative energy – or Karma – round you, which may or may not be neutralised during your current life. If you smoke heavily all your life, and eventually die of lung disease, then you will have reaped what you have sown, and presumably will have had time to reflect bitterly that destroying your body's ability to take in life is not a very good thing to do. But what if you die of something totally unrelated – perhaps in an accident? You will not have neutralised any of the negative energy you have created, which will be added to your overall Karma and *will have to be discharged in some future life.* This would mean that you – the permanent entity which is you – in one or other of your future lives will be drawn to enter a foetus which has a medical predisposition to have any one of a range of lung diseases.

Perhaps in one life you might have squeezed all the love and joy out of your own heart so that you have created negative energy which would have resulted in taking on a heart condition from birth in another life. Or maybe you were so lazy in life that you refused to move out of your chair more than was necessary – and would certainly never walk anywhere unless it was absolutely essential. How would that negativity be neutralised in a future life? Possibly by having an illness which would affect your *ability* to walk, either partially or completely.

We have already said something about how negative thoughts can affect your own health during your current life and, to a certain extent, those who see those ill effects are relatively fortunate, as the illnesses can be traced back to the mindset which has caused them. If this is so, then there is a possibility that by a change of mindset the initial damage which has been done can be either fully or at least partially neutralised during that same life. But when this negative energy is carried over to a future life, there are very few human beings who are capable of diagnosing why a particular child is born with a particular disease – and even fewer who are able to do anything about it.

Let us state once again – by the law of Cause and Effect all actions or thoughts incur consequences, good or bad. *There is no avoiding this law.* Even if a human being seems to have escaped its effects during one life, he will have to neutralise the energy in a future one. Usually, of course, this means that he will have to suffer what he has already caused others to suffer, but in the case of health it normally means that he will have to suffer the conditions which *he himself* has already caused to come into being, due to his actions in a previous life.

So Harry's health will be partially out of his own control: he can do nothing about any predestined illness or disease which he may suffer as a result of Karma built up in a past life. The only thing which he will be able to do is to suffer it with as cheerful an attitude as possible. But what about non-Karmic health matters – the illnesses which have no link with conditions in past lives?

As far as these are concerned, Harry is likely to lead a relatively charmed life, compared with many of his peers, and certainly when compared with poor Tom. As a child he would catch most of the normal childhood ailments, and from time to time he may be affected by epidemics of flu or other such illnesses, but generally he will probably be quite fit. As a youngster he is likely to be coaxed by his parents into doing all the things that medical professionals advise: eating healthily, taking plenty of exercise – certainly in his sporting activities – and avoiding too much excess of anything, and such habits would be carried on into adulthood.

But how about some of the problems that are pitfalls for so many youngsters in your society: smoking, drinking and drugs? Let us say that overindulgence in these areas can usually – although not always – be attributed to emotional problems in the young person's life. Any of them can arise from anxiety or poor self-esteem, which can lead to either succumbing to peer-pressure and doing what everyone else is doing, or taking some substance that may temporarily hide the problem. A young person who is totally self-confident is quite likely to experiment in one or other of these areas, but is unlikely to become addicted to any one substance. Remember that substance-abuse, the overall term for these kinds of problems, is almost always a sign of some deep-rooted need – and normally young people who are emotionally well-balanced are not likely to experience those deep needs.

We should also mention the current problems in your society with eating disorders, which are another manifestation of emotional difficulties. There is currently a cult of *Thin is beautiful* which particularly affects adolescent girls, and much of the rise of eating disorders such as anorexia or bulimia can be attributed to this. Interestingly there are rarely cases of boys suffering from these diseases. Yet the disorder which affects both sexes equally – and a large proportion of your adult population – is that of *over-eating*. Nutritionists have attributed the blame to the fast-food revolution, calling much of what is on offer these days "junk-food," but here again much of the underlying cause is emotional disturbance, leading to what you call *comfort-eating*. There are many medical professionals who now consider the problem of obesity to be a greater threat to the nation's health than any other single factor.

Of course, it is unlikely that our friend Harry will ever have any of these problems, as he is intelligent enough – and emotionally well-balanced enough – to be able to avoid most of the pitfalls which threaten his peer group.

* * *

We have shown what happens to a human being when he reaches the state where he can start to understand what has been happening throughout his many lives, and realises that any negative thoughts or actions will only add further to the amount of Karma which has to be neutralised. Then the whole process of releasing Karma is able to speed up considerably. This is because at that point he is more likely to take active steps to avoid doing anything during his earthly life which will add to that Karma, but also – crucially – he is more likely to take on the burden of clearing as much Karma as possible during the life which he is *about to start*.

So in that new life he could well have multiple problems and drawbacks, which may be concerned with physical or mental disabilities, runs of bad luck, ill-health or relationship problems – or combinations of any of these. Others are likely to marvel at the way that things can go wrong for him, as they observe his apparently wretched existence. But he will usually have one thing in his favour – his mental attitude, which is almost always positive. How many times in your life have you known such people, who have personal lives which are totally disastrous, and yet who seem to inspire everyone else around them with their calmness and wisdom, despite their circumstances.

Some of the people on Earth with the most debilitating physical or mental conditions – or both – are the ones who are the best examples of how human beings should behave towards each other, and that is quite simply because they are very advanced in their understanding of what the purpose of life is. They may not have a conscious knowledge of science, theology or philosophy, but they are still exemplars of *how* to live. And such human beings are almost always at the end of their long journey through the round of human lives, and are nearing readiness for the final release from the journey through the human condition.

Author's Note: *In your New Age language, such people are usually called 'old souls'!*

Of course, to the average human being who prides himself on his rational thinking, the idea of someone deliberately taking on a physical or mental handicap before coming into life will seem ridiculous, but that is because you are all so conditioned to believe that you have only *one* life – the present one – that it is difficult to go beyond that mental framework. Once you can accept the possibility of multiple lives, then things become so much easier to understand: without that leap of imagination there is virtually no possibility of understanding what you call *life's mysteries*. But perhaps it might help if you take the analogy of going to a place of work and having a list of jobs which have to be completed before you can go home. If you make a mess while you are doing these jobs you will have to clear it up – and the sooner that you have finished all your tasks the quicker you will be able to get away. Seen in that context, perhaps it does not appear to be so ridiculous to take on extra burdens in order to finish your transit through earthly conditions much earlier.

11. Children

We now have to touch on a very difficult area – the subject of children.

One animal trait which has been brought over into human life is that of instinct, but in humans this instinct has been expanded greatly to form the basic components of the emotional body. And as the care and nurture of the young is a vital part of the original animal instinct, tied up with the survival of the species, so it has become deeply ingrained in human behaviour. This is why you consider children to be young, defenceless, unable to think for themselves, unable to look after themselves, and needing a long period of time before they are able to cope in an adult world.

This is justified in physical terms as, compared with animal young, children have a much longer period of life before they attain maturity. The length of time which it takes is in many ways a function of the ability of the parents to treat the children as adults: in many societies they are considered mature by the time that they are fourteen, whereas up to fairly recent times in your society they were still children until the age of twenty-one.

But here we are speaking only of the child as a young *human being* – one who is just starting out in life – and that is the only aspect which you can see: you find it very difficult to think of him or her as a being who is continuing a long succession of lives. Even those of you who are capable of seeing yourselves as having a long history of lives in different parts of the world have difficulty in realising that you did not come into this life as a baby entity. You came in as a fully mature entity who happened to have a baby body and was working out a programme of Karmic release. So that many of the things that happen to you, whether as a child or as an adult, *have already been pre-planned for you* – or, as we might say – were predestined.

So all that happens to you is the result of a previous action of your own will. Whatever was in your childhood Karma was caused by your actions or thoughts in previous lives, and you have been drawn into the conditions which will allow you to neutralise your Karma by entering into the foetus when you did.

You may like to meditate on the term *Original sin* in connection with what we have said here? Does it make more sense than the traditional interpretation? Another passage in one of your holy books which could provide food for thought on the same subject is "The sins of the fathers are visited on the children, even unto the third and fourth generation." Does that make any more sense now?

So much attention is being focused on the subject of child abuse – physical, mental, emotional or sexual – in your modern society that you tend to forget that it has always existed. The fact that children are physically, mentally and emotionally weaker than most adults has always made them a prey for those weak individuals who needed someone to use to make themselves feel strong.

However we have to say to you that focusing on *child* abuse is rather like picking out with a pin one of a list of possible human failings, and decrying that while closing your eyes to all the rest. *All* abuse, whether of children or adults – whatever means are used – will bring retribution. And the word *abuse* can just as easily be substituted by the word *exploitation*, which opens up a considerably wider field, including commercial, financial, emotional and sexual exploitation. All of them, when viewed in isolation, can be condemned, but although crimes are easily categorised in human thinking, there is no such ranking from our point of view: the only consideration is of how many people have been hurt, and how much damage has been done to them. This will decide how much Karma has been incurred, and will need to be neutralised.

We wish to take you beyond the human limitation of viewing children as inferior to adults, for there is one way in which they are certainly not always inferior, and that is in their level of spiritual development. The wise parent has always listened to what his or her children have had to say, and many have been astounded by the wisdom which they have produced, far beyond anything they could ever have learnt in the current lifetime. We say *the wise parent*, for the tendency among most parents has been to believe that no child could ever know more than them, as *they* were doing the teaching. The thought of the child having information from any other source was dismissed as ridiculous – and certainly the idea of a child having learned anything in a previous life would be unthinkable.

This is all very important at the present time, as it ties in with what we have previously said about the Earth being at the end of an epoch. In fact there is dramatic change going on everywhere in the galaxy. What it means on a human level is that there are a great number of children being born at the moment who are right at the end of their journey through many lives on Earth. They have amassed a great deal of wisdom about the human condition – having experienced most of it – and also about the place of the human being in the overall scheme of things, within the solar system, galaxy and universe. And these advanced beings have so much knowledge that *even as children* they will be able to teach their parents. Their knowledge, skills and talents will go far beyond anything which the parents have, and they have come into this – their last earthly life – in order to lead humanity into an entirely new way of living. They will demonstrate how it is possible to co-exist with the forces of Nature, with the other species on Earth, and most importantly, with other human beings in order to create a sustainable lifestyle which will be for the benefit of everyone, not just the rich and privileged few.

Names have been given to the successive waves of gifted children who have been born over the last generation – twenty-five years or so – names such as "Indigo children", "Crystal children" and "Rainbow children". These names refer to what appear to be the predominant colour or energy pattern in the child's aura, when seen by psychics. Such children have often been very difficult to understand, as their behaviour has not been anything like that of normal children, as described by the standard textbooks on child psychology. If you have a child who is – or was – difficult to rear it is worthwhile reading one or more of the modern works about the new types of children coming to the Earth.

Author's Note: *See Further Reading under Carroll and Tober.*

12. Karmic Reward

Karma is often called the Law of Retribution and Reward. So far we have been speaking only of the Retribution aspect, and perhaps in doing so we have painted a gloomy picture of the subject, implying that only uncomfortable results will occur because of the working of this law: let us now redress the balance by talking of the opposite aspect – that of Reward.

As there was no question of a judgemental divinity wreaking punishment for misdeeds on a long-suffering and downtrodden human population, so there is also no question of any deity handing out rewards for good actions or thoughts. Through Karma, you reward or punish *yourself*. Because of the law of Cause and Effect, whatever you do to others – whether harmful or helpful – will automatically come back to you.

The timing of what comes back will not always be obvious: sometimes the effect of past actions will be felt during the same life, sometimes they won't. The effects will be able to be felt only if the conditions are right for that event to take place – and that applies in all cases, whether the effects are positive or negative from a human standpoint.

And almost certainly if the effects are postponed to a future life there will be no conscious understanding of why the events are happening. There are some very good reasons for that, as we shall explain a little later.

The Retribution and Reward aspects of Karma are not direct opposites, and the reason for this is that the energy which is produced when harm is done to someone else is a totally different energy to that which is produced when some good is done to them. It is *not* the reverse energy, although to a human mind this may appear so. It is very difficult to explain why, as there are no terms in human language which describe *exactly* these different kinds of energy, so we shall have to do the best that we can by giving analogies. In this explanation we are going to use the words *positive* and *negative* in the way in which you normally understand them – as *good* and *bad*.

We have said that the negative energy which you produce when harming someone affects your permanent self – what we have called the entity – by adhering to it and forming a sort of shell round it which binds the different bodies together, and that is correct. But the positive energy is not the exact opposite of this – it does not do anything to dissolve or loosen that shell. It acts in a totally different way.

Earlier, we gave you two analogies to show how the life force which is all around you is stepped down through your different subtle bodies until it finally arrives, much weakened, in your physical body. You could imagine this in terms of an electrical current being applied to a circuit, and then passing through a bank of resistors until eventually it arrives at an appliance.

If we stay with that analogy for a moment, the effect of negative energy would be the same as adding more resistors into the circuit – it would affect the final output. But the effect of positive energy would not be to remove resistors, it would be to increase the flow of energy *into* the circuit – in other words, it would act at the *other* end. Now this is where words do not adequately convey the full meaning of what we are trying to explain, for the initial energy of the universe is infinite, and nothing that you say or do can ever affect that.

We might enhance this explanation by referring to our analogy of water flowing down a stream, and being gradually slowed down and hemmed in by successive layers of mud. In this sense, negative energy would simply add to the layers of mud, which would eventually all have to be removed before the stream was able to flow freely. But the effect of positive energy would be to widen the banks of the stream *before* it arrived at the muddy section, so that there would be a greater force of water entering that section, which would shorten the overall time which it took to remove the obstacles.

Yet the net result is the same – the positive energy and the negative energy do not directly mix, or have any effect on each other. Viewed from our perspective, negative energy has a very thick, heavy and glutinous appearance, whereas positive energy is an altogether finer and lighter substance.

We hope that this explanation will show that the energies of negative and positive deeds are not in direct opposition. Whatever you do remains in separate *boxes* – you cannot trade off the good that you do against the bad which you have done, and thus get off with a lighter Karma as it just doesn't work that way. To those of you who are commercially-minded, it is like having two separate accounts in the same bank: whatever you put into, or take out of, either one has no effect on the other.

But the *effects* of positive and negative energy *are* diametrically opposed to each other in one way, in that the negative energy binds the subtle bodies together, stopping the entity from being released until everything has been neutralised. On the other hand, the positive energy, which works with the positive and harmonious aspect of the primal energy source, has a beneficial effect in helping that primal energy to flow with less hindrance through the body so that the person can achieve understanding of the whole process much sooner, allowing the permanent entity to be freed from the human condition more quickly.

* * *

So what, then, are the benefits in everyday life of doing good deeds and of thinking kind thoughts about others? Well, to start with, we must consider what we understand by good deeds which will attract positive Karma. In our vocabulary, these are defined as things that will help someone else to live a happier and/ or more fulfilled life. But there are several provisos here, because you do not necessarily help someone by giving them what they want: a child may want to play with fire, but you certainly wouldn't help him by giving him a box of matches. It would be of far more value if you taught him why playing with fire is not a good thing to do.

In the same way, you wouldn't help people who were addicted to drugs or alcohol by giving them money – which they might immediately spend on buying more of what was harming them. And if you gave money to a shopaholic or a gambling addict who has run up large debts because of their addiction it would soon disappear in the same way. Once more, it would be of far more value to them to try and help them to overcome their addiction.

Author's Note: *As a general rule, it is not usually of much help to a person to give them money: if they are in financial trouble, find out how they got there, and then possibly help them to overcome the conditions which caused the problem.*

The channelling session continued:

But what if you do a paid job which helps others, such as providing a counselling service, or working in a hospital, or doing some other sort of social service: does that count as doing good? Surprisingly, No! If you are employed to do a certain job, do it to the best of your ability, and are paid for it, you have merely done what is required of you, what you are under *contract* to do, and as such there is no particular connection with the law of Cause and Effect at all. So the type of job you do does not directly affect your score for good deeds. Of course, if you don't do the job to the best of your ability you are cheating your employer, and so incurring *negative* Karma!

Those who enter into a caring profession usually have a basic desire to help others, and very often do far *more* than is expected of them in their work, and if this is the case their actions would certainly come under the heading of doing good. It is only when someone does a job mechanically, just going through the routine in order to earn money, that they acquire no added value for their actions.

So now we had better define *good deeds*. You do a good deed when you do something over and beyond what is required of you, with the intention of making someone's life more pleasant or tolerable, and with no intention of getting any benefit for yourself out of what you have done. If you examine that sentence, it immediately opens up all sorts of possibilities: for instance what is, *over and above what is required of you?*

It means that whatever you do, in your dealings with others you try to be as kind and helpful as possible. Let us take for example the cases of two people who are nurses in a hospital. Both are equally skilled in their profession, but one treats all the patients as numbers, and does what has to be done in an air of cold efficiency, without any thought for the patients' mental or emotional needs. The other one is just as efficient, but sees every patient as an individual, and talks and laughs with them while giving them their treatments. Which one do you think the patients prefer? And which one is doing good – over and above what is required?

The second proviso is *with the intention of making someone's life more pleasant or tolerable*. This states that the primary aim of what you do must be to help the other person – and it acknowledges that the other person may have far more needs than merely physical actions could satisfy. For instance, a friendly smile or a kindly word may mean a whole lot more to a lonely person than any physical action possibly could.

The third proviso is *without any intention of getting anything for yourself out of what you have done*. There are so many people in your modern world who are quite happy to do services for others – providing that they themselves are making something out of doing so. When this happens, even in the best cases, there is no positive Karma which comes from those actions – they are merely different examples of what we have called *contract* above. In the worst cases, the whole intention of the persons doing the services is to gain benefit for themselves, regardless of the effects on those whom they are *helping*. We are sure that you can all think of examples of helpers who have defrauded their charges out of large sums of money. In all such cases, of course, there is likely to be a substantial Karmic *debt* incurred.

With an understanding of what *good deeds* mean in the context of Karma, we can start to examine the different implications of what you do in your everyday life.

Let us imagine an extreme case of good deeds: you are walking along a river bank when you hear cries from someone who has fallen into the river, and is obviously in difficulties. *Without thought of your own safety* you immediately dive in and rescue the person. What is the result of your action from the Karmic point of view?

To start with, you are likely to receive praise and thanks, not only from the person whom you have saved but also from his/ her relatives and friends. That will affect you in two ways: first, the thanks will be positive energy, which will increase your capacity to receive the primal energy of the universe, as we have pointed out above. But interestingly it will make you feel good about yourself, and that will have a positive effect on your own aura, and will make you feel more confident. This in turn will be picked up by those in your environment, who will be more inclined to react favourably to you than before. To reinforce this feel-good factor, it is quite possible that your brave act will be reported by the local media, so that for a short time you may become a local hero.

That is obviously an extreme case, and very few people will ever have the opportunity of doing something as impressive as that, but before we move on, let us tell you of another side-effect which is not immediately obvious. At the moment when the person was struggling in the river, there was obviously quite a high probability that he or she would drown, but you, *by an act of will,* ensured that they survived. You have dramatically changed the initial reality of that situation, and have replaced the *probability* that they would drown by the *possibility* that someone would come along and rescue them. You may remember that we spoke earlier about the fact that the primal energy force contains all possibilities, and how by a concentration of repeated thoughts you can push a certain one up the ladder. Well, you have done more than that – you personally have actually changed the final outcome of the situation, and in doing so *you have left a permanent imprint on the energy field at the place where it all happened.*

This permanent imprint will of course be unnoticed by the majority of human beings, but those with high sensitivity will be able to plug into the event long into the future. *Every* action leaves an imprint on the energy field where it happens, and if you could only develop a machine which was sensitive enough you would be able to go back in history and *read* what has happened in any particular place.

This may sound ridiculous, but how many of you have walked into a building which you have never visited before and felt either fear or foreboding. Psychics can certainly sense the atmosphere of places where crimes have been committed; many of them, in different countries all over your world, are able to help the local police to solve various crimes, usually of missing and/ or murdered persons, by using this same ability. You even have television programmes devoted to what you call "ghost-busting" – so the possibility of an action imprinting itself on the atmosphere of a place is certainly not unknown to you. When an unnatural death occurs, through a murder or a tragic accident, in many cases the human victims involved are so tied in with the energy of the place where it has occurred that their subtle bodies are unable to free themselves without help, and they become earthbound.

But let us go back to your heroic action which we mentioned earlier. For a time you would bask in the gratitude and glory of your action, and then, as the memory faded, the additional boost which had been given to your aura would wear off, and you would be back to where you were prior to the incident. But not every part of the effect would wear off. We mentioned that the positive effect of good deeds is to enlarge your ability to receive the flow of primal energy. In order to do that the positive energy attaches itself to the interface between the primal energy source and your mental body, and its effect would remain with you for the rest of your life. And it would stay with you after the end of your physical life, as part of the permanent entity which remains after the dissolution of the physical body and its interface.

Few people will ever have the opportunity of doing anything heroic in their lives, so what advantage is there in doing everyday acts of kindness? Every advantage – even more than there is in doing large and spectacular good deeds! Let us imagine that you are the kind of person who is always doing little good deeds for neighbours, friends or even strangers. Strangers? Yes, why not? We are not talking of anything extraordinary here, but a smile or a kindly word when someone else is in need is just as effective to a stranger as to someone whom you know. It is interesting, in this context, that in at least one of your human languages there is a saying to the effect that "a stranger is a friend whom you haven't yet met."

Now if you do a good deed to someone, apart from sometimes getting thanks for that deed, you will feel a little bit of satisfaction for having done it. This might not be conscious – it would be better if it weren't conscious – but it will exist. Then, if another good deed is done, either to the same person or to someone else, the same thing will happen, and the original bit of *feel-good* will be reinforced. Soon, on a subconscious level, you will start to sense these little bits of self-satisfaction, and this will raise your own self-esteem slightly. In turn, this will have an effect on your aura, and will help you to give out a more positive energy, which other people will start to pick up.

When this continues over a period of time, the action of doing good deeds for others starts to become a habit with you, and the more that it becomes a habit, the more you will do it. We hesitate to suggest that you become *addicted* to doing good, as that word has rather negative connotations, but it is a similar situation: you do it because you *like* doing it, and this increases your enjoyment of life itself.

There are some human beings who do good deeds just for the personal gratification of showing others how advanced they themselves are – a *holier-than-thou* attitude – but in these cases there is little Karmic benefit received. About such sanctimonious people one of your holy books says that "they have their own reward" – in other words, the only actual benefit that they receive is that of emotional self-gratification. But in many such cases the individuals are given the rather derogatory epithet of "do-gooders," which rather defeats the object of their exercise of showing others how good they are. A different quotation advises you "not let your right hand know what your left hand is doing" – in other words, do your good deeds quietly, without ostentation.

But starting to enjoy doing good is not the only benefit which you gain: remember that we said that the positive Karmic energy has the effect of increasing the flow of primal energy into your whole being, by attaching itself to the interface to the mental body. As the flow of primal energy increases, it stimulates the development of the mental body and promotes a greater understanding of *what* you are and *why* you are on Earth. The increased knowledge, what we could call *illumination,* has a practical effect in that the greater energy pouring into the mental body brightens the aura of the person involved, and this once more means that they become far more sought after and more highly-regarded by those whom they meet, socially or in a work situation.

But the increased benefits do not end there. Once people are living and working in harmony with the primal energy force, they start to be able subconsciously to *affect* that force, and draw to themselves increasingly beneficial possibilities which, through the force of their personalities, they are able to move up the ladder in the same way as if they were consciously directing thoughts in order to do so. In many cases they reach the state of harmony where they *expect* things to be always for their ultimate good – one of the last stages before being able to *control* those possibilities, which is often called manifestation.

Here we should clarify something that arises out of what we have just said, and which may be misunderstood. In some societies there are certain practices which exist in order to *force* beneficial effects to happen for the sole benefit of the individuals concerned: such practices are usually called *Witchcraft*, *Black Magic*, or *the Left-Hand Path*. All of these practices have one thing in common: they attempt to impose the collective will of the followers in order to sidestep the natural law of Creation, that of Cause and Effect. It goes without saying that any attempt to avoid the law is doomed to failure, and will incur very heavy Karmic debts in many lives to come.

Contrast this with the constant repetition of good deeds for your fellow human beings: here you will eventually become so in harmony with the primal force of the universe that agreeable and beneficial circumstances will eventually be drawn towards you *without you even consciously asking for them.*

There is one final beneficial aspect of reaping positive Karma, and that is in the realm of health. Your medical researchers have made enormous strides in understanding how the human body works over the last few decades, although much more work still lies before them.

Over the last few years many of the more advanced researchers have come to the conclusion that human physical health is somehow connected with mental and emotional health – they use the term *psychosomatic* – and in this they are perfectly correct. Thoughts are things, and the thoughts which you have about yourself and your body, and the emotional experiences which you have had during your life can have an effect on your physical health. Where these thoughts and experiences are negative, the fact that many of the effects are delayed for decades does not mean that they are any less serious – and may in some cases prove even fatal.

It is a great pity that there is still a great divide between scientific research and spiritual knowledge: if scientific and religious thinkers could only agree to pool their respective fields of expertise they would probably find that jointly they could make enormous strides in the alleviation of human suffering. Perhaps in this little book we may be able to excite the imaginations of some of the more liberal thinkers on both sides so that they join together in future collaboration.

Perhaps there are some of those same liberal thinkers who may be able to stretch their minds out and encompass the scenario which we have put forward:

1. that the human being is far more complex than you had ever imagined,

2. consisting of several non-corporeal bodies

3. and interfaces which form the connection between the primal energy

4. – the life force of the universe

5. and the physical body.

If this could be fully understood then some startling discoveries would be possible which would dramatically alter what we have called *the human condition.* For instance, some inspired researchers have even postulated the possibility of a human blueprint which keeps under control the individual atomic structures making up the human body. We congratulate them, but suggest that they might consider the possibility of what we have already put forward. There are *three* blueprints, which we have given the name of interfaces: the first one is the blueprint of the mental body, the second the blueprint of the emotional body, and the third the blueprint of the physical body, and *all* of them have a regulatory function. Perhaps if they can pursue this line of thinking they may be able to solve some of the more mysterious aspects of human health on all its levels.

13. Prayer, Health and Healing

Since we have been considering various aspects of health, perhaps it would be appropriate to look at the subject of prayer and health. Let us start by saying that prayer exists in all civilisations, in all religions and even among those who do not profess any religion at all – although such people would probably deny this. Perhaps in its simplest form prayer means an expressed wish to change a particular reality, and that might be widely acceptable, for everyone tries to change reality at some time or other during their life. It need not be about a health matter, it could be about a situation, a relationship or even about the weather, but we will confine ourselves here to considering the health aspect.

As you will recall, this is our basic premise:

1. that you are a being who is made up of particles of energy,

2. and your physical body is swimming in a sea of energy.

In order to create the physical body, there has been a need to gradually increase the density of the particles, in order to bring down their vibrational rate, and this has been done by creating a set of different bodies and interfaces, until the last interface has been of a low enough vibration to link with the physical body. We have pointed out that there is an interaction between the different bodies and the physical body, and have shown how imbalances in the mental or emotional bodies can cause conditions leading to physical illnesses of various kinds.

Here we would ask you to consider what the possible effects of might be transplanting an organ from a dead body into a live person, to replace a defective one. Remember that the dead entity had *crafted* a special interface to join its emotional body to its physical body, and if an organ is removed it is likely to take with it the appropriate part of the interface connected with that organ. So what happens when it is introduced into an *alien* body? The interface of the alien body will react against the intruder, and try to reject it. In extreme cases – for instance in some heart transplants – even when the rejection has been controlled by drugs, the transplant recipient has started to feel some of the emotions which the donor originally felt.

This is not a diatribe against organ transplants – they are extremely useful medical procedures which have saved many thousands of lives. But if you can understand the *reason* behind the phenomenon of organ rejection, it could give you a pointer towards alleviating the problem. The problem is on a *psychic* level which, due to the interconnection between the various subtle bodies and the physical body, shows itself in the physical body. So you need to overcome the problem on a psychic level, through psycho-spiritual healing.

We do not suggest that you abandon your current anti-rejection drug therapy in favour of psycho-spiritual healing. But in the cases where drugs are not effective against the rejection, and the physical body is dying, it might be a wise move to call in the services of a healer. Is there any medical specialist who, faced with such a situation, would be prepared to risk his/ her reputation by doing such a thing? Or even would they be prepared to introduce the healer at a much earlier stage in the process, giving a greater chance of success? Interesting questions. We can only give you the facts, and leave the rest up to you.

To return to our main theme, if you have a particular illness, the best person to help to alleviate that illness is – yourself. There have been many studies done on the effect of what you call *bio-feedback* which, in its simplest form, is a way of altering physical conditions by using the power of the mind, mainly through visualisation techniques. As we said about using the power of your mind to change reality, within the sea of primal energy there are all potentialities, every possibility of an outcome of every course of action. These may be thought of as being in an ascending ladder of likelihood until, at the top, there is the one which is most likely, which we have named the probability.

We suggested that by the power of concentrated thought it is possible to move a possibility up the ladder until eventually it reaches the top and becomes the probability – and this is true. We do not suggest that it is an easy procedure, for two main reasons: one is that there has to be the *will* to achieve the result – and part of that will is the belief that it *can* happen. If you start with the idea that such a thing is impossible, it is not very likely that you are going to be successful. The other reason is that it needs a great deal of *concentrated* thought, and few human beings have the habit of focusing their thoughts on anything for more than a short period of time. This can be less than a minute in most cases – unless intense concentration is an essential requirement of their profession.

Both of those conditions are equally necessary if you are trying to improve your own health, but there are other considerations as well. Before you came into your present life, because of the Karma that you had accumulated from previous lives, you were drawn towards the foetus which had certain predispositions to a certain kind of existence, and one of those predispositions concerned your health.

In order to learn certain lessons to do with good health, it is first necessary to experience what poor health means. If one of the goals of your present life is to learn a particular lesson about health, so long as you have still not learnt that lesson, then your health will not – and *can* not – improve. If you could change it by a simple act of will, then you would in a way be side-stepping your lesson, which is not possible.

This is most obvious where the primary health problem is one of physical or mental handicaps, and in this case there is virtually no possibility of changing the condition. We say *virtually*, as in one or two very rare cases such a thing has been done, but in each one the circumstances were so extraordinary that the possibility can for the most part be discounted. But, as we stated previously, those human beings who take on these conditions in a life are usually so advanced in their spiritual journey that they probably would not choose to change their path anyway.

But let us assume that your current health problem is not Karmic: how can health be improved merely by the application of concentrated thought? Everything in human life is subject to the overall law of Cause and Effect, and nowhere is this more obvious than in matters of health. Mental and emotional states are very often the triggers for physical health problems, but in many other cases there are *physical* triggers for various diseases and illnesses. These may range from those which are obvious to everyone – from pollens, smells or materials which cause a range of allergies – hay-fever and asthma, for instance – to the body's inability to adequately process certain kinds of food. Dairy products and wheat derivatives are the most common issues here, but there are many others. In extreme cases there have been reports of people with an allergy to nuts who have died from the reaction to eating one mouthful of a food which contained nuts.

When you are suffering from an illness, or more probably from a long-standing health *condition*, by concentrating your thought upon getting better you are plugging into all of the possibilities concerning your own health – and one of these possibilities is that the condition is caused by what we have outlined above, mental or emotional conditions, allergies, intolerances or other physical causes. You will not consciously think of these possibilities, of course, as your only thoughts will be about the final outcome – of becoming well again – but as you are moving *that* possibility up the ladder you are also moving the possibility of finding out what is *causing* the problem up the ladder as well. After all, the two things are so closely linked together that you cannot achieve good health without first finding out what is causing your bad health. Eventually, you may reach the state where you realise that becoming well cannot be achieved without finding out the cause, and concentrate on that. Once it happens, *that* becomes the higher possibility than becoming well and overtakes it on the ladder, and finally becomes the probability.

At that point, the way of finding the cause may well manifest itself, in one of a number of ways. You could read an article in a magazine or newspaper about allergies or intolerances, or be drawn to a book about the links between emotions and physical health, or have a conversation with a friend who mentions a case very similar to your own. The result of any of these things might be that you

a) will be impelled to find out more,

b) will eventually come to a conclusion about what is causing the condition, and

c) will do something about it..

Once you start to do that, then very quickly your primary objective in concentrating your thoughts on getting better could well become manifest – and *you* will have brought it into being.

* * *

Sometimes there are other techniques which are more effective – for instance the technique of visualisation. Here, you visualise – see in your mind's eye – the result which you wish to happen as if it had already happened. For instance, if you are a man with an enlarged prostate, you could well visualise the prostate as being the size of a large apricot, and will it to reduce in size for several minutes. We have mentioned the problem that many people have with concentrating for more than a minute, but the wished-for result is worth the mental discipline required. Then on successive days you could do exactly the same exercise, and imagine it slowly reducing in size. It might help to put an imaginary ruler behind the apricot so that the difference in size could be measured. After about a fortnight you could possibly note that the symptoms which you have are becoming less severe, and after several months you might have considerable relief.

The same technique has actually been used in holistic therapy to reduce the size of tumours, and in certain cases claims have been made for a complete cure. The medical term for such occurrences is that the condition is *in remission* – but no one yet has been able to explain why spontaneous remissions occur in some cases and not in others. Perhaps if more research were done into the effect of mental states on the prognosis for various illnesses a pattern would begin to emerge. We realise that there have been a few random studies which have been carried out, but there has been nothing done systematically over a wide range of illnesses.

May we put forward one very good reason why the mental state of the patient is of vital importance in the consideration of disease? When most people have an illness, they worry about the likely outcome, and almost inevitably they fear the worst. For some reason this seems to be a general trait among the members of the human race. It seems to be more comforting to think of the least favourable outcome as being the most likely one: perhaps this is so that when the final outcome is known – which in most cases is not the one feared – then a sense of relief can be justifiably felt – and enjoyed. You even have a saying that "A pessimist is never disappointed." We would suggest that all that negativity being generated by and around the patient – because obviously the relatives are worrying too – will affect the possibility of an *unfavourable* outcome, and push it up the ladder – and in extreme cases it could make it become the probability, with dire results.

Contrast this with the sort of person who is always positive, who accepts that there will be illness from time to time, but believes that the eventual outcome will be favourable every time. In this case, he is always pushing *that* possibility up the ladder – and the likelihood is that he will usually be proved right. Not only will that person probably be free of most serious illnesses for most of his life, but also – even more important – he will live a happier and more peaceful life, free of the needless worries which he might have had if he was of the opposite disposition. Always remember that the vast majority of the things about which you worry in life will never happen, so why cause yourself needless stress?

On the subject of worry, let us show you how two different individuals may react to a known fact, with totally different results. The only indisputable fact in *your* life is that one day you will leave the physical body, or *die*. You may react to this in two different ways, as demonstrated by our two subjects:

Person A is so obsessed with the fact of his own eventual demise that he worries about it continually, reads every kind of health article he can find – in the process finding out a lot of diseases which he previously knew nothing of, and which now give him more cause for worry. He has a vast range of so-called elixirs and tablets which he takes daily, and when he eventually dies at the age of 94 he has endured ninety-four years of Hell – or almost Hell.

Person B is quite aware that he will not live forever – and then promptly forgets the fact, and gets on with his life. When he is actually ill, he takes steps to remedy the problem, and as he grows older – and more problems become apparent – he takes the advice of health professionals and takes whatever medicine is suggested. He also dies at the age of 94, having not necessarily lived ninety-four years of Heaven, but having certainly had that many years of *life*. Which of our two subjects would you rather be?

We started by saying that we would talk about prayer and health, and at this stage some of you may well be asking why we haven't yet mentioned prayer in the way that you understand it – the idea of imploring the favourable intervention of some celestial being, god, saint, angel – or whatever is appropriate in your own particular religious tradition. The reason is quite simple: *you* are living *your* life, you are the *only* person who can live that life, and so you are the best person to bring – or at least to try to bring – changes into that life. And without an active concentration of thought from you it is not likely that any celestial being *would* bring a favourable change into your life.

This thought may upset those of you who are devoutly religious, and doubtless you will cite cases where some celestial being has actively intervened and produced a miracle cure. But we would suggest that if you study each of those reputed cases you will find that the intervention has only followed after an expression of *will*, either by the patient or by someone acting on his/her behalf – and there is a very simple reason for that. Each of you is living out your life with the subconscious intention of neutralising all or part of the Karmic negative energy which surrounds you, so that eventually you will be able to move on from Earth conditions in order to learn about other planets, solar systems, galaxies, and universes.

If any celestial being intervened in your life *without being invited*, then they would be altering your destiny in a way that only *you* can choose to do. And by that action, the cosmic law of Cause and Effect would have been broken – which is not allowed.

But before we go on to discuss the ability of celestial beings to affect your life, let us finish what we were saying about health by asking if it is possible to heal another person. This is an interesting question, as in your modern society you are beset by large numbers of people who claim to be able to heal others in various ways, by any means from the laying on of hands to the use of machines, crystals, oils, scents, sound or drugs. (Here we deliberately refrain from commenting on orthodox medical practices.)

The first thing to do is to repeat what we have said above regarding interfering in the lives of other human beings, and to state that *no* human being can heal another. Once more, there has to be an expressed wish by the patient for healing to be given, in whichever way, and without that *express* wish, then there is no possibility of healing taking place. But provided that the patient is willing to be treated, is it possible for another person to heal him/her? Once more, the answer is, "No!" – the healing must come from him/herself. Let us explain this by reference to the most commonly understood kind of healing – the laying on of hands.

When a healer – usually known as a contact healer, as they normally place their hands on the patient – gives healing to a patient, the healer him/herself connects with the primal energy source and directs it to wherever there is a deficiency on any level. The primal energy is positive and will automatically be drawn towards the deficiency, which is negative. Now the primal energy is not coming *from* the healer, it is coming *through* the healer, and so the healer is acting merely as a channel, a duct through which the energy flows. In some religions the healer is referred to as *the instrument* to distinguish between the energy which is flowing and the healer's physical body. So if healing actually takes place, it is because the patient has received a dose of primal energy to overcome the deficiencies within the subtle bodies which reacted on the physical body and caused the illness in the first place. Once those deficiencies have been remedied, and the subtle bodies restored to normal functioning, then the physical body is automatically brought back to health once more.

* * *

Exactly the same thing applies, whatever method of healing is used. If, for instance, the healer is using a system of massage with aromatic oils, then the primal energy is in the aromatic oils, and as they are soaked into the skin, so the primal energy soaks into the subtle bodies, once again targeting the areas of deficiency. The energy does *not* come from the healer. There is obviously benefit from the action of massage on tense muscles, but that is only incidental to the final healing which may or may not take place. If the healer is using crystals, then the primal energy comes from the crystals, and not from the human being. In all cases of healing, the healer is merely an intermediary: in some cases the energy flows *through* them, in others it does not, but in no case is he or she more than a facilitator.

Author's note: *The same reasoning would be used when the healing is done through the use of Homeopathic remedies: the energy comes from the remedies themselves. However, as continued dilution moves the vibration of the remedy nearer to that of the primal particles of the universe, paradoxically greater dilution gives greater potency!*

The channelling continues:

So now we move on to consider the importance of prayer as a means of achieving healing. Let us say at the start that there are a huge number of celestial beings of all sorts; you are aware of only some of these, while you are totally unaware of the existence of others – more about that later. Let us confine ourselves for the time being to talking about the types of celestial being of whom you are actively aware. Some of these will have led documented lives as human beings, while others will have never had such lives. In the first category are listed gods – such as the founders of some religions – prophets and saints. In the second are listed gods who have never had an earthly existence, and various demi-gods, archangels, angels and similar beings. So what is the effect of prayer addressed to such beings?

When you are praying for an improvement of your own health, you are invoking the help of one or other of these beings, and asking that they should change your present reality. But these beings are themselves part of the initial primal energy – the more religious of you would say that the gods *are* the initial primal energy – and so what you are doing is contacting that primal energy and asking that it should cure you. You are *connecting* yourself with that energy, and if the time is appropriate for you to be healed, the deficiencies in your current subtle bodies will be neutralised and that will lead to a healing of the physical body. Where healing does actually take place, the most important part of the process has been the connection between the patient and the energy. The patient has had an *act of will* to connect to the energy, and this has led eventually to the healing.

Now this act of will has been given several names in different religions: the most common one is the word *faith*. Indeed, in one momentous act of healing mentioned in one of your holy books the patient is told, "Your faith has made you whole." The use of the word *faith* has generally been understood to be about believing in the particular religion or god. We would suggest that its true meaning is, *believing in your ability to connect to the energy*. In another quote from the same source, people are told that if they had enough faith they would be able to move mountains – which certainly does not mean believing in that particular deity.

Human beings have difficulty in thinking of energy in abstract terms. It is far easier to think of a celestial being as having all energy, power, might – call it what you will – than it is to believe that that energy, power or might could exist in isolation. So it is far easier for a human being to call on a god, saint, angel or other spiritual being rather than to attempt the mental exercise of trying to contact the energy directly.

But in the final analysis, it does not really matter what your belief system is: whether you are calling on your god, an angel, a saint, or whatever other being may be appropriate in your religion, *you are making contact with the primal energy* – and that is the most important thing.

But for the sake of those who deny the existence of any such supernatural beings, and believe that the human being is potentially all-powerful, when they are using any of their own inner powers to try to affect a cure for a particular illness, they also are connecting to the primal energy – *and have just as much possibility of success as those of a more religious persuasion*. This may seem like blasphemy to the religious – but it is the *Truth*. This is why we said, earlier on, that when humanists and atheists do such things they are actually indulging in *prayer* although they themselves would never think of using the term.

Earlier we said that healing could take place *if the time were appropriate*, so you are entitled to ask, "When is a time appropriate and when is it not?" We have already stated that if you have a particular illness or long-standing condition which is Karmic, and has been brought forward from a past life in order for you to learn a certain lesson, then that condition or illness will remain until you have completely learnt the lesson which it is teaching – and until that situation is reached there will be no possibility of healing. It is possible that it will take a whole lifetime for all of the negative energy which has been brought into your life by the condition to be neutralised – you cannot know. But as soon as the time is ripe, then a cure will take place. This will explain why some people spend a lifetime praying for an illness to be healed – and get no result – whereas another person with a similar illness is cured after one prayer session only – the so-called miracle cure. There are no miracles, in the way that you understand the term: there are only specific applications of laws of which you do not know or which you do not yet understand.

The other thing which we must think about when we are considering whether or not the time is appropriate, is the case of terminal illness. When an entity chooses to come into life as a human being, it does so with certain aims in mind, aims such as the lessons which it wishes to learn, the contacts with those from previous lives which it wishes to renew, and – crucially – *how long the lessons will last* – i.e. how long the life will last. When all the lessons of a particular life have been learnt, and when all the tasks which were planned have been accomplished, then the entity is *allowed* to go back into the dimension from which it came – in other words, the physical body dies.

Now from a human point of view, you do not see things that way at all. All you see is that you have a loved one who is terminally ill, and you want to prolong their life, so that you can have the pleasure of their company a little longer. But that is not what the entity wants at all. (Remember that the word *entity* is the term which we are using in order to distinguish the eternal, permanent part of the human being from the physical body and its interface, which will rapidly disintegrate on physical death.) The entity has already decided when it wants to separate from the physical body, and no matter how strong are the bonds which the person has with the family and friends – or even how much the person may *consciously* wish to stay in life – that decision is paramount, so there is no possibility of prayers from loved ones delaying the timing.

But what about prayers for the wellbeing of others? First, you must remember what we have already said, that no person can heal anyone else, or interfere to change the pathway that such a person has *chosen* to follow. So is there any point in praying for the health of another at all?

The answer is "Yes!" – but not for the reasons which you may imagine. What you are really doing, when you pray for the health of someone else, is expressing loving thoughts about them, and as we have explained, thoughts are things, and capable of changing reality. The thought which you send out either *to* them or *on their behalf* will direct primal energy to them, and thus will reinforce their own connection with the overall primal energy. So you will be acting in a similar way as if you were giving them healing, in one or other of the ways we have described above, and will be reinforcing the possibility of them recovering from the illness – or moving that possibility up the ladder.

* * *

Let us now consider prayer from a different viewpoint, when it has nothing to do with the expression of a desire for the betterment of someone's health. For instance, is prayer of any use when trying to improve a particular political condition, or to bring peace into a war-torn area? In this, we have to return to what we said about someone who wishes to change a situation in their own life, who by concentrating on the situation, and particularly on the desired outcome, is able to influence the order of all the possibilities, and move the desired outcome up the ladder. We pointed out that it takes a great deal of concentration and directed thought, but we suggested that in certain circumstances it is possible to successfully change the reality which currently exists.

Now there is little difference in essence between that scenario and the will to change a political situation somewhere in the world: the only difference is one of scale. It is very unlikely that any one person could change something on a national scale, but that doesn't mean to say that it couldn't be done at all. It would just need more people to do it. For instance, there had been repression of black people in the area which you call South Africa for many generations, when suddenly it changed *almost overnight*. What caused the change? There were many factors involved, but one was that large numbers of people throughout the world had been actively praying for change to happen for a long time – many decades – and this certainly had an effect, pushing the possibility of change up the ladder until it became the probability. Another example was the situation in the area which you call Eastern Europe, which had been under the domination of another country for almost half a century. Once more, people all over the world had prayed for a long time for the liberty of each of the subordinate states, and then suddenly – dramatically – it all happened.

This is another example of the misuse of the word *miracle*: many people thought that the sudden collapse of both of these regimes which we have cited was *miraculous* – but they did not see what had been happening in the background for so many years which led up to the final changes.

It is possible to change almost anything in your world by the use of a concentration of directed thought: you can stop wars, genocide and tribal conflict, changing behaviour patterns to something which is far more positive and acceptable – *provided that enough of you make the effort*. Obviously the ways that you do this will be many and varied, ranging from formal prayer groups in religious gatherings to informal direction of thoughts for peace in private meditation, but it can be done. Actually, at the moment we are quite optimistic about the future for you, as more and more of you are realising that thought and prayer can change realities in your world, and the more this is known the greater effect it will have.

Author's Note: *Nothing in this chapter must be taken as a reflection on orthodox medicine, or as a suggestion that advice should not be sought from orthodox practitioners.*

14. Planetary Change and Human Survival

Although you could change a great deal in your world by a concerted effort of will, there is one thing which cannot be affected by you now, and that concerns the physical changes which are coming into your planet at the present time. You are actually coming to the end of an Age – in planetary terms – and there are enormous changes ahead of you, changes which will affect every one alive at present. You are already starting to be concerned – a little tardily – about the effects of *global warming*, but you are incorrect in assuming that global warming can all be attributed to Humanity's activities. When two things happen simultaneously, it does not necessarily mean that one is the direct cause of the other. Your present planetary weather is part of an overall cycle of weather patterns which has affected your Earth for many millions of years, and you are certainly not yet at the level of technical competence to be able to do anything about *that*. Perhaps, on reflection, it is a good thing that you are starting to be concerned about how to do something to stop the ravages of Humanity upon the planet: it may well start you along the path of thinking how the human race is going to survive in the years which lie ahead.

* * *

If you were able to review the history of your planet over a period of many millions of years, you would find that there have been many disasters which have wiped out almost all the life-forms at one time or another. You are aware of some of them – for instance the cosmic disaster when Earth was struck by an asteroid, leading to the end of the Age of the Dinosaurs – but there have been others of which you have no knowledge at all. Much work has been done by your scientists, who have found puzzling indications connected with changes in the magnetic polarity of the planet. You are aware of what you call Ice Ages, and can plot the extent of coverage of ice in your Northern hemisphere over a period of several thousand years but there are still enigmas like the discovery in icy climates of extinct animals who, at the moment of their physical death, were still eating vegetation which grows only in a temperate climate.

Such a situation is now imminent in your world, and will entail just as much devastation as previous cataclysms have produced, with a similar effect on the life-forms which currently exist in it. As far as Humanity is concerned, there will be a mass exodus of human beings – we will enlarge on that later. You would call much of it *a loss of life*, but we prefer to say that the majority of those currently on the planet *will make their transition*. The greatest effect will be in the highly industrialised areas, and that is where the greatest loss of life will occur. Paradoxically, those *primitive* communities who are still living a largely hand-to-mouth existence in agricultural conditions will fare best, as most of the complex structures of your advanced urban civilisations will be physically destroyed in the devastation. This will leave the few human beings who still exist with the task of basic survival in a world which is completely different to anything which they have known.

All of this is in the overall pattern of evolution of the planet and all its inhabiting species, and is totally natural. As far as human beings are concerned, those who are left to start the re-population of the new world will *have* to work with the forces of Nature in order to survive. So a new realisation will be implanted in the minds of all that the current selfish attitude of exploitation of the resources of the planet could not continue without the prospect of mass extinction of all the life-forms on it. Also, since in the new order of existence co-operation will be vital if communities are to survive, it will be seen that the exploitation of the majority of people for the benefit of a select few will be impossible – for without the skills and talents of *all* working together, *none* of them will survive.

So are we being too alarmist in repeating this information? Not at all, for many of you have already reached this conclusion, and know that each of you is an entity which is eternal, developing and evolving all the time. During this evolutionary process, you will make many mistakes which will add a further amount of negative energy to your overall being, and all of this accumulated negative energy will have to be neutralised before you are able to leave the influence of the planet and move on to further adventures in other realms, worlds or dimensions. Each of you has come into this life with an outline plan to learn certain lessons, which will neutralise a specific area of accumulated negativity within you, and in doing so will move you nearer to your eventual goal.

Part of your individual life plan concerns the time and the way in which you will die, and when you arrive at that time you *will* leave your physical body, regardless of what you – in the conscious mental state – your family, friends or colleagues wish at the time. You will leave your body because *you* – as an eternal entity – have *decided* that it is the most appropriate time. Once you can understand that fact – and it *is* a fact – then whether you die peacefully in your bed, through an accident, as a result of a crime or in some major cataclysm is of little importance: it is what *you* have decided.

It will not have escaped your notice that in your modern world there is a great deal of violence, not only caused by human beings but also caused by Nature. We have already spoken of the implications of human violence – the law of Cause and Effect – but if we consider for a moment the violence shown by Nature, we will see that there is a pattern in it – and it is growing. There are more natural disasters, floods, tidal waves, volcanic action and storms, and year by year these have a greater impact on human life. The reason for all this is that there is a quickening of pace as the Earth comes to the end of a cosmic age, and the energies affecting it from across the galaxy are becoming more pronounced and powerful.

* * *

You are daily being reminded of the damage which the pollution of your species has caused to the planet itself and to many of the other species which co-inhabit it. Only recently you have started to realise that the waste products of your lifestyle have caused death and destruction to so many other life-forms, and the latest evidence of that is has been presented to you in the form of horrific pictures of how one of the materials which you have created – plastic – has caused agonising death to many marine and airborne creatures.

It is now much too late for you to do anything about the present state of pollution which exists – even if the concentrated will existed to create a co-ordinated plan to do something about it. Regrettably, because of the fragmented state of your society, where even your world organisations are unable to draw together the disparate aspirations of individual nation-states, you cannot even come to a consensus of opinion about what action to take regarding what most of your scientists consider the foremost threat to life on your planet – global warming. How much less then are you ever going to be able to agree to clean up the pollution which you have collectively caused over the last century or more of industrial growth.

So the massive clear-up which will be necessary in the future will have to be undertaken by a power which is much mightier than any of which you currently have conscious knowledge – and this is the power which binds you into the universal network of life. Others have spoken earlier of the force which led to the creation of the universe and different galaxies and star systems, and have explained that everything is ultimately connected together at a level of the particles which are the building blocks of all forms of manifestation, but we would like to tell you a little more in order to expand your understanding of this connection.

You have heard that you are totally surrounded by these particles, which form the primary energy source, and were given the graphic image of how you are a small island in an ocean of energy. Each one of you, individually, is part of the energy pattern of your immediate surroundings, and thus of the overall energy pattern of the planet. You were told earlier that you are quite capable of influencing the flow of this energy by an active concentration of thought, and this is perfectly correct. However, every thought which you ever have, and certainly every action, disturbs the flow of energy to some extent, so that all other beings – which are also part of the overall energy pattern – are indirectly affected.

Now once you can understand that basic fact, then perhaps you can also accept that just as you have your own little local energy pattern, so – on a much larger scale – does your planet have its own pattern, which fits into the pattern of the solar system, which in turn fits into that of your galaxy, and so on. So whatever you do, as an individual, will have an effect in some way on the whole of the universe. Some of your scientists have already theorised on this interesting fact by coming up with the tantalising image of the beating of a butterfly's wings in one place causing a cyclone to happen on the other side of the planet – the so-called *butterfly effect*. We congratulate them, but suggest that they now consider the logical extension of their theories to the behaviour of individual human beings insofar as it concerns the universe as a whole.

We can tell you that the cumulative affect of what Humanity has been doing over the last century, culminating in the use of atomic energy for both military and industrial purposes, has already affected the energy pattern of your whole planet, and is beginning to affect the pattern of your solar system, causing an imbalance. Since the primary law of Cause and Effect applies on all levels of manifestation, even on the universal level, that imbalance has already created the opposite – neutralising – energy, which is currently building up and will fairly soon result in a massive surge of energy flowing through your planetary atmosphere, with unimaginable consequences for all the life-forms in your world.

The planet itself, which is of course a life-form in its own right, will survive the impact of the storm, although in a much different form. Parts of continents which now exist will disappear, and others submerged for millennia will come to light, and although some parts of Earth's surface will remain relatively unchanged, the future map of its physical features will be quite different – although still recognisable.

So what will be the impact on the life-forms of the planet? Well, of course the predominant life-form is your own, so that is what we will consider first. Those of the human race still on the planet at the time of the storm will suffer massive loss of life, and will in many areas be totally wiped out, although the effect will not be evenly felt over the whole surface of the globe. There will be pockets of land where there is hardly any change whatsoever to the physical landscape, and in these areas the inhabitants will stand a good chance of survival, but in most areas – at least in those which are not totally submerged after the storm – there will be few buildings left standing, and even fewer human beings surviving. Overall, we estimate that less than ten per cent of the current population will survive the physical changes – and far fewer the changes in the energy levels of the new order.

As far as the animal population is concerned, surprisingly they will fare far better than human beings. Of course, those in the land masses which disappear beneath the sea will not survive, and those in the relatively unaffected pockets of land will survive just as will the human populations. But to a large extent the survival of the remainder will depend on their size: the larger animals will fare badly, and many species will be totally wiped out, but the smaller ones will be far less affected. Remember that in the mass extinction of the dinosaurs small mammals were almost the only survivors. As far as insects are concerned, they will be relatively unaffected, as will the majority of marine life-forms. Since human beings have become the greatest danger to many of the current species, the majority of these will adjust rapidly to the new situation, and within a relatively short time will breed so prolifically that the seas will once again teem with an amazing variety of marine species.

The life-forms that will be least affected are those of the vegetation. Humanity has often marvelled at the ability of Nature to repopulate the Earth after natural catastrophes such as floods, bushfires and even volcanic action, and this will be the case once again, with one difference. In the past century, much of the vegetation on the planet has been badly affected by the activities of human beings, who have tried to impose their domination by large-scale deforestation and the use of poisonous chemicals. Once this activity has all stopped, there will be a luxuriant flourishing of all kinds of plants and trees, which will dramatically alter the look of the land. Many areas – those which are newly emerged from the sea – will be considerably slower to become fertile again, but within decades will have overtaken those areas which have been unaffected, and will show a much wider variety of plant life than elsewhere. The areas which will take longest to readjust are, of course, the concrete jungles of your cities, but within a century or so most of these will have totally disappeared under the relentless and unchecked growth of the invading vegetation.

*　*　*

Let us be a little more specific about the situation which your planet is currently facing. We will remind you of what was said previously about the phenomenon of lightning, which is caused when the electrical charge in storm clouds and the opposite charge on the ground builds up to such an intensity that the tension between the two *has* to be resolved: it is resolved when there is an exchange of energy between clouds and earth, seen as lightning. In a similar way, there has been a tension of violence building up in the planet over the last century – cosmic influences are slower in effect than human influences – and this has now reached the point where the forces of

Nature are being unleashed with increasing frequency, leading to the final resolution (the lightning effect). Natural phenomena such as earthquakes, floods and extremes of temperature, which were rare occurrences in your recent history, have now become commonplace, and even volcanic action is becoming more frequent. All this is part of the change which is taking place, and is a forewarning of what is to come.

You are able to predict with a fair degree of accuracy the weather patterns for any particular area in the immediate future, and with slightly less accuracy for up to several months ahead, but this is done by measuring the data which is already available to you on Earth. However, these almost imminent changes are on a cosmic level, and although you have on rare occasions suffered catastrophes of cosmic origin in the past, you have no means of measurement which will allow you to calculate the precise timing of the cosmic storm which is about to take place. And this is of benefit, because if you did it would generate mass hysteria throughout your world as the appropriate time approached.

However, I can reassure you on one or two matters: first, the event will happen so quickly that there will be no time at all to worry about it. Those of you who have chosen to end your current life in the flesh at that moment will suddenly find that you have already left the body, without knowing that it was happening. I remind you of what was said earlier, where animals in a temperate area were suddenly, within minutes at the most, frozen stiff, while still having fresh vegetation in their mouths. Of course, not all of those who die will have this happen to them, but whatever will be the cause of their demise will be just as rapid.

Next, since in eternal terms there is no such thing as time, as you understand it, there will be no point in anyone making detailed plans for survival. On previous occasions when there have been forecasts of doom, people have built themselves underground bunkers and filled them with large stockpiles of food, in order to survive the impending holocaust – which never arrived – but on this occasion there will be no possibility of doing that. This is because you will have no warning whatsoever that the storm is about to break – and you would certainly not have time to get into your bunker, even if you had one.

But there is another, far more cogent, reason to be reassured, and this is that you have *already* decided – before you came into this life – when you will leave it, and if – for you – it is during this impending storm, then no matter what you do consciously, or how much you worry, it *will* happen. If, on the contrary, you have decided that you will survive, then *that* will happen, whether or not you have tried to make any preparations, or whether or not you even think about the matter.

Those who do remain on Earth will be faced with far more difficult times ahead than they could at present imagine. You are currently used to living in an extremely complex civilisation, surrounded by creature comforts to such an extent that any interruption of what you consider is your *right* is the cause of great indignation.

Possibly you could do a little mental exercise in order to imagine what it will be like for those few hardy individuals who survive and who are faced with the job of trying to construct a new life from the ruins of the old one. Just imagine a world without any of the services to which you are accustomed; no electricity, gas, water supply, sewage disposal, food, transport or housing. You currently bandy about the phrase *the New Age*, but do you realise what that really means? It does not mean the setting up of new forms of governing to lead society into a golden age of living, complete with all the creature comforts which you currently have. What it really means is creating a new society from scratch, going back to the roots of communal living, working together not because you *want* to but because you *have* to.

For those true *New Agers* it will mean concentrating on the most important things of life to the exclusion of all others – how to survive, build your own dwelling, grow, gather or hunt your own food. It will mean stable relationships will become vital, as the present climate of virtually limitless choice of casual partners will no longer exist. It will mean teaching your own children the skills which they will need in order to survive. It will mean finding the true meaning of *love* in caring and sharing relationships with all others within their community – and that means *everyone* – from the young to the old. It will mean that everyone has his or her job within the community, and that the death of any one of them will be a tragedy to all.

Paradoxically, perhaps, it is the old people in the new communities who will be best off, as they will have the knowledge of what used to be done in less technological times. They will increasingly – as communities develop – be seen as repositories of wisdom, and as such will be more and more revered, as opposed to the current situation in many of your societies where to be old is to be unwanted, unloved, and merely burdens on society.

At this point, you may raise the objection that we are speaking as though the present population of the world is no more advanced than primitive humans were hundreds of thousands of years ago. Not so! We accept that the general level of knowledge is far in advance of that in those days, but knowledge without the skills, materials and facilities available to do any particular job of work are of little value. In many ways, the primitive tribes currently in your world are far more advanced than you, as they are able to live off the land, look after themselves and flourish without the interference of *civilised* men, whereas without the trappings of your current civilisation, how many of you would be able to survive in the wilds?

But, you will say, why are you talking about going back to the wilds? Surely there will be much of the current civilisation available for the survivors to inhabit and use? To answer that, we have to tell you more of what is going to happen: to start with, there will be a massive magnetic storm, such as has never been experienced on Earth before. This will lead to a reversal of the current magnetic poles (your scientists have already noticed dramatic changes in the magnetic fields round the poles). Then there will be an imbalance which will occur in the area of the South Pole which will affect the current stability of the Earth itself, and will suddenly trigger a crustal slip, in which the hard crust of the planet will slide over the more fluid interior, and re-orientate the whole physical geography of the planet. The stability of the continental plates themselves will be affected, and the results will be the simultaneous triggering of hundreds of volcanoes, some of them dormant for thousands of years. The violence and speed of the crustal movement will cause winds to rage over the surface of the Earth, reaching speeds of several thousands of kilometres per hour, and the combined effect of all these phenomena will be that most of the man-made structures on the planet will be obliterated – and with them all of the facilities on which you currently rely to operate as an industrialised civilisation.

Faced with such a situation, you may well feel that those who have already chosen to leave their human bodies at this time will have the better deal – and in earthly terms this is certainly correct. However, the final bit of reassurance that we can give you is that none of you need to worry about where you should go in order to give yourself the greatest chance of survival: those of you who have already chosen the difficult path of helping humanity to re-establish a new order will be impressed to move to wherever they are meant to be at the moment when it all happens. Some will be taking a holiday, others will have been impressed to move house, or will have relocated to another part of the country – or indeed, to another country – because of the demands of the organisation for which the main breadwinner works. Others, who happen to already live in the area where they are meant to be – one of the *safe* areas – will be impressed to stay put instead of going away somewhere during that year.

Author's Note: *This process has been going on over the last two decades, and is now largely complete.*

The channelling continues.

But whatever the situation, and whether or not you are to survive to help on the difficult task ahead, you will be in the *right* place, at the *right* time, with the *right* people and doing the *right* work, to prepare you for what is to become of you. So many of you know and use the phrase *to go with the Flow*, and yet so few of you really understand it. It means that you understand that everything is totally perfect in the working of the universe: there are no *mistakes*. Even what you think of as mistakes in your ordinary everyday life are usually seen to be not mistakes at all, when viewed with the benefit of hindsight – but of course, you do not appreciate this when you have to work through the painful lessons at the time.

Going with the Flow also means that you are prepared to work with the universe – co-operate with the flow of universal energy, in order to create the *New World*, for which you so often yearn. And when you are prepared to co-operate totally, without reservation, you will realise that there is never any need to be concerned about the future – all will happen for your eventual benefit.

Author's note: *This chapter, when taken alone, seems to indicate that the vast majority of the human race is doomed. However, the text is explaining what will happen during the planetary cleansing process only. A later part of the channelling considers the whole scenario, before, during and after the planetary ascension, and gives a far more comforting view.*

15. The Life of the Universe

We have said that Love forms the building blocks of the universe of matter, created in an unbelievably massive explosion. We will explain how – and why – this happened, but first we must repeat what has been said before: everything which exists, either in a form which you can understand or not, consists of minute particles of energy. These particles are so immeasurably small that many millions of them could be packed into a single atom. But each particle is also a minute unit of *intelligence*. We understand that it is very difficult for you to understand the concept of intelligent energy, but this is what you will have to try to do, if you are to grasp what we are about to tell you. In fact, certain of you have already touched upon the idea in your study of Quantum Physics, when you have realised that what is done in one location can have an effect on something else in another, even when the two locations are far apart. Some of you, possibly braver than others, have theorised that it is possible for the particles to communicate with each other, which implies some degree of intelligence, does it not? If you can push the boundaries of this idea, then great discoveries are not too far away.

Although these individual particles are independent, they are also capable of taking concerted action, either on a localised or on a general level. When acting on a localised level, they are capable of forming and holding the identity of an object. Take a plant, which is made up of roots, leaves and flowers. Each aspect of the plant's essence dictates its ability to create the whole.

Although each intelligent particle is independent, it is always in connection with every other one, and this has far-reaching implications. The reason is that the particle is part of the localised life-form, but that in turn is part of the next level of organisation, and so on. The plant's structure is dictated by its environment, which in turn is dictated by its localised climate, country, continent, planet, solar system, galaxy, universe – and of Creation in general. And if we consider that the particle is a unit of intelligence, it follows that each of those larger units is also a form of intelligence, and finally – dare we say it – that the whole of Creation itself is an overall form of intelligence. One of the stock sayings of your New Age movement is based upon the Hermetic maxim, "As above, so below." But no one yet seems to have realised that the corollary of this is "As below, so above" – which is equally valid.

Throughout the ages, Humanity has had ideas of the intelligence of Creation, and this has given rise to an enormous number of theories about what it is, where it came from, and how the act of Creation took place. From time to time advanced beings have been born to put forward explanations which have formed the basis of new religions.

When someone is prepared to look beyond the specific events and characters which are involved in the theology of individual religions, and consider the basic principles behind those events and characters, it will be realised that there is a remarkable consensus of opinion about the nature of Creation itself, and the way in which it came about. In fact, it would be quite possible to extract many of the sentences from most of the sacred texts and implant them into others, without there being any sort of obvious disagreement in context. And this fact is both relevant and important as we go back to our discussion of the events which led up to the Big Bang.

In the beginning there was Energy, intelligent energy, consisting of an infinite number of particles – and that was all that existed. All of the particles were in continuous communication with each other, so that in fact they effectively constituted a single intelligence. All was calm, peaceful, unchanging. But after untold aeons of time, the intelligence became restless – using words which convey human emotions is the only intelligible way in which we can describe what happened. It wished to expand, it wished to experience itself, it wished movement. But expansion of the whole intelligence was impossible, as it stretched to infinity, so the only thing that could be done was to expand a small section of itself. This also was difficult, as a simple expansion would just merge with the surrounding energy and have no effect whatsoever. So what was done was for the section to *contract*, sucking in energy from its immediate surroundings, and becoming increasingly denser, until it reached the limit of the possibility of concentration. At that point, the addition of even more energy caused a reaction – the explosion which you now know as The Big Bang.

The explosion created, for the first time, what you now call matter, but it also did something else, which is quite fundamental in your universe: it created polarity! In the original state of energy, polarity was impossible, as the original energy was totally homogeneous. No opposites could exist in a state where everything was uniform, where all particles were completely identical. But now, in the new state of affairs, particles were grouped together in different densities, and the difference in density gave rise to polarities, which had to balance out in order to maintain the overall structure of the universe. Some of this balance was achieved by the fact that the matter was flung in all directions at once, but a large part of it had to be achieved in another way. Some of the particles had become clumped together in matter which was relatively heavy, whereas others became matter which was relatively lightweight – once again we use human terms of explanation.

Author's note: *the original word was "light," but this has been changed to "lightweight" to avoid possible confusion when the word "dark" is used later.*

The channelling continues:

So to achieve balance, there had to be far more lightweight matter than there was heavy matter, and overall the weight of the heavy matter was almost fifteen times that of the lightweight matter, which meant that there had to be about fifteen times as much lightweight matter in order to balance it.

Obviously, we have greatly simplified a very complex subject, as the concentration of particles did not fall into two discrete densities, lightweight and heavy. There was a wide range of densities in each category. But we have used simplified terms in order to explain something which has been a source of concern to your cosmologists, who have proved that the basic mathematics of the universe does not add up, using only the facts which you currently have at your disposal. We have used the terms heavy and lightweight to indicate the division between what is solid enough to be sensed with the equipment and instruments which you now use, and that which is too ethereal to be currently sensed. We believe that you currently use the term *dark matter* to denote what is not immediately apparent, and you have correctly theorised that such matter must exist in order to stop the universe tearing itself apart. In this you are approaching the concept of what we have called balance.

When you make further advances in the sensitivity of the instruments which you invent you will find that, just as there is a wide range of densities in the matter which you *can* currently identify, there is a similar wide range of densities in the dark matter, which you can *not*, and in the near future you will discover a type of heavier dark matter which will further your understanding, reduce the apparent error in your mathematics and – incidentally – prove the validity of what we have just explained.

* * *

However, the factor of balance did not stop there. Whatever matter was created had to have its reflection in the opposite of created matter – created non-matter – or *anti-matter*, as you now call it. And there is just as much – in fact, *exactly* as much – anti-matter in the universe as there is matter; this is not in doubt. At the moment you do not have the instruments to detect this, although your theoretical mathematics prove that it must exist. In fact, you have been able to produce minute amounts of it in laboratory experiments, but far too little to prove its qualities. The only thing that you know at the moment is that it is so diametrically opposed to matter that should minute amounts of each come into contact they would produce an enormous explosion, and both would be instantly transformed back into pure, stable, concentrated raw energy.

If you could harness the vast energy produced by the collision of just one atom of matter and one of anti-matter, you will produce an enormous supply of energy for every purpose. However the technology which would be necessary for you to do this exists only in the minds of some of your most inspired thinkers, so for the time being the prospect must be viewed as only a distant dream. The realisation of that dream could only take place when humanity as a species was sufficiently advanced to be able to use the resultant energy solely for peaceful purposes – and if you look around your world at the moment you will have to accept – however grudgingly – how distant that future is.

Before the Big Bang event the only things which existed were particles of intelligent energy, and these were distributed in a uniform fashion throughout existence. Once more, there could be no differentiation between any part of whole and any other part, as that would have created a turbulence and upset the homogeny of the whole. But once the Big Bang had happened, and polarity had appeared, all of the rules were changed. There was now no homogeny, but a vast variety of differences; and as we have said, one of the differences was a difference in densities between separate states of being.

One of the interesting results of all of this was that what you now know as the Law of Attraction appeared. This, in human terms, means that there is a force between two separate bodies which is capable of drawing them together. You see it in all facets of life, from the area of human relationships to the attraction between two planetary bodies.

There are different ways in which the Law of Attraction may occur, but what is it *in essence*? Quite simply, it is exactly the same thing occurring on a particle level as occurs on every other level. When particles occur in different densities in separate pieces of matter, the particles in the matter with lower density will be attracted to join those in the matter with higher density. This will not happen all at once: the particles at the edge – once more a human description – will be attracted first, and will join those at the edge of the other matter, marginally altering the balance between the two pieces of matter, and rendering the denser one even more dense and more attractive. This then attracts other particles to cross over – and so the process continues.

But at the same time that this is happening, the particles in between the two pieces of matter are also affected. There in no vacuum in between anything in the universe. Particles exist, in different densities, in every part of it, even in deep space. Let us take the example of the air on your planet, which is composed of a mixture of several gases. Each of the atoms of these gases contains enormous numbers of particles – far less than the atoms which make up what you call physical objects, but still enough to amount to many millions per atom. So how are these particles affected by the migration of particles between the two pieces of matter which we are considering?

The intelligence within each particle recognises the intelligence within the particles of the other – denser – piece of matter, and that recognition creates a force – an energy (*kinetic energy*) – which impels it to move towards the other piece of matter.

As the movement of particles from one piece of matter speeds up, they attract the neutral particles in between the two pieces of matter, which reduces the particle density between those two pieces, and when this has carried on for some time the density has been so reduced that the lighter piece of matter is drawn towards the other in order to close the gap and re-establish the original density between the two pieces. Then the whole process is repeated, and even speeds up, as the two pieces of matter are drawn closer, until eventually they come together and form one single piece.

* * *

Over a period of time – a vast period of time in human terms – the force of attraction started to overcome the initial force of the explosion, which was – and still is – hurling the original particles away from the point of origin at an immense speed, and the differentiation of densities caused by that explosion became even more marked. But it was now enhanced by the fact that particles of anti-matter were attracted to particles of matter, creating new explosions which sent particles in different directions from those of their original trajectories, and creating a more random appearance of the distribution of visible matter. This has meant that now, many billions of years after the event, when you try to understand the nature of the universe there appears to be no perceivable pattern at all in its structure.

This has led to much discussion in your scientific community regarding the size of the universe, whether it is finite or infinite, and of its possible future development over the aeons which are ahead. Will it continue to expand, or will it reach a point where the initial momentum is exhausted, and it falls back in on itself? The former theory is reinforced by the fact that the matter at the edge of detection by your current instruments seems to be accelerating in speed, even allowing for the distortion caused by the fact that they are at an awesome distance from your planet – so great, in fact, that you are *now* seeing them as they *were* many hundreds of thousands of light-years ago. So what can we say about the eventual future of the universe?

The first thing to say is that the number of particles in the universe is *not* infinite. You will remember that we said that although the original number of particles which made up all-that-was-in-existence was infinite, only a small proportion of these were used to create the conditions which gave rise to the Big Bang. In human terms, considering that there are enormous numbers of particles in each atom of matter, and that there are an incalculable number of atoms in the universe, it may well appear that there is no end to the number of particles which exist, but that is not true. The number is finite. So what does that fact tell us about the eventual destiny of the universe?

Once more we will give a human analogy: in order to demonstrate the fact that the air which you breathe has a certain density, it has long been a standard scientific experiment to extract all the air from a metal container, and to show that when the pressure of the air in that container falls below a certain level, the pressure of the air outside it will crush the container. From this you prove the adage "Nature abhors a vacuum." (You say that "Nature *abhors* a vacuum": it would be more accurate to say that "Nature *compensates* for a vacuum.") Can that fact help you to understand the eventual fate of the universe as you know it?

A similar situation will eventually occur within the universe: the fabric of its being – the matter and anti-matter which it contains – will at some remote time in the future become so stretched that the number of particles in its centre (the origin of the Big Bang) will become progressively reduced to a condition where they start to tend towards zero, to use one of your mathematical terms. We should point out that this has been happening since the original moment of the Big Bang, and has never ceased to happen, but that process itself can not continue indefinitely. At some time, the density of particles will become so small that the matter immediately round the original location of the point of origin will start to be attracted *back* to where it came from, to prevent an absolute vacuum occurring, and once this process starts to occur it will be the beginning of the end for the life of the universe. As the central point becomes more and more attractive, and pulls in more and more matter in order to normalise the situation it will take on a life of its own, and will then continue to attract matter even after the vacuum-like conditions have disappeared. This will increase the local density to such an extent that it starts to swallow up everything in its immediate vicinity – and will do so at an ever-increasing speed.

An interesting phenomenon will occur here: we have said that when your original universe was created by the Big Bang, balanced amounts of matter and anti-matter were created, and because of the force of the original explosion they were flung widely apart. Since that time small amounts of each have come together and created localised explosions, which have had the effect of sending matter off in different directions, but now we must point out another effect of these explosions. Whenever matter and anti-matter come together, not only do they explode, but they are instantly converted into *pure energy* – the same form of energy as that of the original state of being, so that from the viewpoint of their effect on the physical universe, *they no longer exist*.

Consider the effect that that will have on the process which we are describing:

The situation at this time will be that there will be an enormous, and ever-increasing, density at the point of origin which is pulling in matter to itself by the force of attraction, and it will pull into its vicinity a certain amount of matter and anti-matter at a particular point in time. Depending on the concentration of each, they will come into contact at a certain distance from the point of attraction, and will create an explosion which will send matter in different directions, and affect the timing of its eventual reunion in that point. However, by this time the force of attraction will be so great that the explosion will only delay that reunion – it will not be able to stop it. But of far more importance to the whole process will be the fact that both the matter and anti-matter which have been combined will no longer exist – in effect creating a small localised vacuum – and that localised vacuum will accelerate the drag on the physical matter which is being drawn towards the density. So the force of attraction will increase exponentially – as will the speed at which the whole universe collapses in on itself.

But you may well ask what will be the difference on this occasion from all the other localised areas of extreme density which already exist, and which have the same sort of attraction on all surrounding matter. In fact, many of them have such an attraction that they can even stop light from travelling away from the area concerned. There is one major difference which will distinguish between those densities which already exist and this new density which will come into being and signal the end of the universe: its position. In all other cases, they are in areas which are *receding* from the point of origin of the Big Bang: in this case, it will be *at* the point of origin. In the former cases the full force of the phenomenon cannot be experienced as it is lop-sided, to use a human term. In the case which we are describing, it will be situated so that it has a balanced effect in all directions, and will be able to draw in matter from all directions at once with equal force.

It is not possible to describe accurately the force which this centralised density will have – it will be so immense that all words will fail to give even an approximation of its power. But when we say that its force will be great enough to attract and swallow up even those other densities in other parts of the Universe to which we have referred, your cosmologists will have some idea of what we mean. It will be strong enough to slow down, halt and reverse the direction of all the celestial bodies at the edges of your known universe – and of many other bodies currently unknown to you – and hasten its demise. As for its speed of working, we have stated that this will increase exponentially, so that the whole process from start to finish will be completed in a small fraction of the time which has existed since the time of the Big Bang until your present era.

But let us now consider another factor in the whole process, that of the elimination of matter and anti-matter. As we have stated, when matter and anti-matter collide and explode together they are returned to their primeval state of pure energy, and as such cease to exist in a physical form at all. Since everything in the universe consists of either one or the other form, and in quantities which are exactly balanced, as more and more of each is attracted to its opposite – and eliminated – there will be less and less which remains in the universe as a whole, until in the final analysis, when the last amount of anti-matter is attracted into the density, it will create another – final – Big Bang, with the difference that this time it will be one in reverse. The original one brought the universe into being, the final one will take it out of being, and restore the pristine situation of pure energy, peace, harmony – call it what you will – which existed before the start of manifestation.

So what will happen after the end of your universe? No one knows – and when we say no one, we mean neither those currently in human form, those like us who were formerly in human form, or those beings who have never had a human existence. In the tradition of one of your religions, it is said that the life of the universe is like the breathing of the Creative Force: at the moment you are in the period of the in-breath, when everything is expanding. There will be a time which we have described when it will be the out-breath. Thereafter, the whole process may start again – or may not. Some of your scientists have theorised that as the universe contracts and becomes infinitely dense, this will itself *cause* another Big Bang, but as we have explained this is not possible. It will not become *infinitely* dense due to the increasing effect of matter and anti-matter neutralising each other and reverting to pristine energy. There may eventually be another Big Bang, or there may not. If there is, it may happen immediately, or after an indeterminate time of several billion years. All will depend on the *will* of the Creative Force, the collective particles of intelligent energy from which everything originally came, which may – or may not – decide to repeat the experiment.

16. Dimensions and Dimensional Travel

You have already been given some information on the event which you call the Big Bang, and have been told that it created a situation in which particles were able to come together in various densities and form what you understand as matter. You were told that there is a wide range of densities, some of which are detectable by your scientific instruments and others which are not. You were also told that all Creation conforms to the law of Balance, and the working of this law in your own universe has been outlined.

We now have to enlarge on that theme, and explain that what was created was far wider, and far more complex, than anything which you can currently comprehend, for all human beings – with the exception of a few highly specialised scientists – are used to thinking in terms of *one* universe: the one which is apparent to your senses. However, we have to tell you that your universe is only one in a number of universes. But as the others – and their characteristics – are currently inaccessible to you, we will confine ourselves to talking of your own universe only, and when we use the word universe we will be referring specifically to the word in your everyday sense, meaning what you can see or sense in the space surrounding your own solar system.

Within your universe there is a range of different dimensions, although the way in which we use the word dimension is slightly different to the way in which you normally use it. When you use the word you speak of your world as being the third dimension, as everything can be measured in terms of length, breadth and depth. Some of you also understand a fourth dimension – that of time, and others go as far as to talk of higher dimensions still.

You have been told that the essential building blocks of all creation are minute particles of intelligent energy, which is true. Now all energy has a specific vibration, and the vibrational rate of the primary particles is at such a high level that if you took your highest figure currently used in mathematical calculations and multiplied it by itself, you would not even approximate to that rate.

You were told earlier that the Law of Balance requires there to be as much matter in the universe as anti-matter, and have been told that the amount of matter which you can currently detect must also be balanced by the matter which you cannot, but which you can prove mathematically must be there. But that same law applies, not only to your own immediate dimension, but to others as well. Now a dimension is really a band-width of similar rates of vibration, and so in the whole of Creation there must be a balance of dimensions round the central point, or average band-width.

It may be of value to think of Creation as being like a gigantic see-saw, with dimensions strung along it from left to right, the lowest on the extreme left, the highest – the primary particles – on the extreme right. In this scenario, your own dimension would be third from the left.

Now in each dimension there is a set of circumstances which is totally different to that in every other. Since the rates of vibration differ so widely, life does not exist in the same way in each: even the word *life* is a total misnomer – a far better and more accurate word would be *existence*. And as for life-forms, very few humans are able to conceive of more than a minute fraction of the life-forms in your own universe, which you can see, so there is little possibility of most of you visualising what exists in other (higher) dimensions, which you can not.

So if other dimensions are so hard to understand, can they see and comprehend your own world? Here, we must say that not only they can, but they do, in far more ways than you could possibly imagine – and we will explain why and how.

* * *

The vibrational rates at the very top end of one dimension are not very much lower than those at the bottom end of the next one, although there is always enough distance between them to form a barrier. You are not normally aware of life-forms, or of events which happen in the fourth dimension, and in the same way we – who are currently in the sixth dimension – are not able to experience what is happening in the seventh.

However, it is much easier to perceive what is happening in dimensions below those in which one currently is, and travel down and up again is relatively simple, for two reasons. The first is that one already knows what conditions are like in the lower dimension, and the second is that one is taught how to do it by those who are already in the higher dimension and have mastered the techniques necessary – and this happens to everyone on their first introduction to a higher dimension. This is why we are able to visit and inspire you so easily now.

In cases where a high-level spiritual being has to descend into your earthly world for the first time, it is quite a complicated process to go down through a series of dimensions. A human analogy would be when a deep-sea diver has to spend a long time in a decompression chamber in order to bring his body through a differing range of pressures before coming back to the pressure of the surface – except that in the case of the celestial being it is necessary to do the reverse and *increase* the density as it passes down through the dimensions.

So are human beings able to visit and experience the next dimension? Yes, in various ways. Firstly, the fourth and all higher dimensions are *mental* dimensions, and every human being has a mental body, which is formed of material of a vibrational rate which is the same as that of the fourth dimension. So by going through certain exercises which temporarily release the mental body from the emotional and physical bodies – for instance, through practicing yoga or various forms of meditation – a state may be reached in which communication with that other dimension is possible.

These are practices which are commonly used in a religious context, or for religious purposes, but any form of intense mental concentration may provide a trigger for a spontaneous inspiration or enlightenment, as many scientists have discovered.

Some people are born with an innate gift for contacting the next dimension, and these people are normally called psychics. They may decide to use their gifts in later life as mediums or healers, but many are content just to use what they call their intuition in order to help them to get through the problems of their daily lives more easily.

Many of those who have these heightened psychic abilities, particularly in primitive societies, choose to develop them through a long period of training in mental disciplines, and on occasion part of the training is the use of specially-selected drugs in order to release the consciousness in a controlled way and allow the person to travel mentally into other dimensions. Where this happens the person is usually known, and practises, as a shaman. The difference between a medium and a shaman is that the medium receives information from discarnate beings who come from another dimension, whereas a shaman actually travels into that other dimension in order to bring the information back.

All these are ways in which a person may choose consciously to experience other dimensions, but there is one way in which all human beings may experience those dimensions unconsciously, and that is in sleep state, i.e. through dreams. When someone is asleep, their conscious mind is turned off, and the effect is exactly the same as when they practice yoga or meditation – scientists who study sleep and dreaming have found out that the measurable activity of the brain is very similar. During sleep state, the mental and emotional bodies are capable of roaming at will through time and space, so that sometimes the person has a dream of being in another part of the world, sometimes of being in a fantasy world, and sometimes even being with long-dead relatives or friends.

Meeting with these relatives or friends may be explained by saying that they still exist in another dimension, but it would be more difficult to explain how people may have prophetic dreams during which they see events happening in the future – events which then happen in reality. How can that be explained? One way to look at it is to realise that everything in your human world exists as a potentiality, and previously we have mentioned a ladder of possibilities, with the probability of any outcome being at the top of the ladder. Where someone has a prophetic dream, they have merely seen and experienced the probability which is at the top of the ladder.

* * *

It is an interesting fact that all human beings have a basic need for sleep, and various scientific experiments have proved how devastating sleep deprivation can be. Certain cruel regimes in your world have refined sleep deprivation into a torture which is capable of deforming people's minds to such an extent that they can be induced to confess to any crime at all, even one which they were physically incapable of committing.

However, we return to our study of ways in which human beings can visit other dimensions, and here we must mention the one most frequently used – the practice of taking so-called recreational drugs for purposes of self-gratification. This practice has always existed in your world, but in your current society, with the growth of modern means of transportation, it has become a veritable epidemic, affecting the lives of many millions of your citizens in ways which are beginning to threaten the very fabric of society itself.

We will not comment on the medical and social effects caused by drugs, which are already well enough documented: we will only mention the one side-effect of drug usage which is almost completely unknown to you, and that is the long-term psychic harm suffered by drug users.

When the human being dies, the physical body and its organs cease to function, and eventually disintegrate. All do not cease to function at the same time, which has led in the past to interesting ethical discussions about the definition of when a human being can be considered to be technically dead.

Once the physical body has died, there is no further need for the interface which preceded it, and so that also rapidly ceases to exist, and dissolves into its own constituent particles. This means that all that is left of the original human being is the discarnate and bodiless life force, the mental and emotional bodies and their respective interfaces. You have already been told why these are left, and do not dissolve in the same way as the interface between them and the physical body. We have given the name *entity* to the amalgam of what remains of the human being after death.

Here is the important part: this item or entity is what forms the blueprint for the future human being, as it contains all the memories of everything which has happened to date. You may be confused if we use the word *memories*, because that has a fairly precise meaning in human vocabulary: perhaps we should use the more correct word *energies*, as everything which you think of, say and do has an energy. Where those energies are harmful they attach themselves to the subtle bodies, and stick to them until they are eventually neutralised by having the opposite energy applied to them.

So the blueprint is the thing which will decide what the future human being will be, as it will automatically tend towards trying to enter conditions which will allow it to neutralise some of the harmful energies, from past lives as a human being, which are currently polluting it. A simple analogy in human terms might be that when you have been engaged in some strenuous exercise, and have become very hot and sweating, you will at the first opportunity want to have a shower or to take a bath to get clean again. Of course all of the energies which have become accumulated over many human lives cannot be simply washed away in a single life, but the overall principle is still the same.

But, you may ask, why is the abuse of drugs any more harmful than that of other substances such as alcohol? When you use alcohol, it alters your level of consciousness for a short period of time only, whereas the use of drugs will alter that level *permanently*. It is a matter of degree. If someone drinks excessively and gets drunk, the effects soon wear off after a night's sleep. Their mind and emotions may have been altered for a period of time but there is no permanent damage. Even when someone is an alcoholic, and continually craves the kick which they get from drinking, the effect on the mental and emotional bodies will be relatively shallow and reversible. We do not intend to belittle the dramatic effects that alcohol abuse can have in the lives of those who are addicted and their families, but we point out that it is almost always possible to reverse those effects through psychotherapy and counselling. Drying out alcoholics has become quite a booming business in your modern world.

But when someone uses drugs, these have an immediate effect on the emotional and mental bodies of the person, and that *does not heal up* after a good night's sleep. It remains as an area of damage in those subtle bodies, and can not be healed by any physical or mental means. An analogy in human terms would be that there are certain toxins which the body can deal with and throw off relatively easily, whereas there are others which cannot be processed, and become cumulative and eventually fatal. In the same way, additional use of the same drug will increase the amount of damage in the same area of the subtle body concerned which will in time become so damaged that – to use human terms – holes will appear in the psychic fabric of the body. Further use will create so many holes that, to someone who is psychic, the fabric of the subtle body will appear to be badly torn – which will have a harmful effect on the blueprint, and on future lives.

* * *

We can now consider the two dimensions which are below you in the dimensional hierarchy, and the entities which inhabit these dimensions. Both of the dimensions are non-physical, which means that they cannot be detected by any instruments which you currently have available, and so the entities which inhabit them are in non-physical forms.

In the following analysis, we will use the words *entity* and *entities* many times. We realise that we have already used the word to describe the permanent state of a human being, but we are now going to describe other *entities*, both beneficial and harmful, so for clarity we will stick to the following definitions from this point on:

1. Soul: the complex group of particles which band together with the intention of experiencing life on Earth as an individual human being, and which remain together before, during and in between successive lives on Earth.

2. Entities: discarnate beings which are harmful to humanity.

3. Spiritual Beings: other life-forms which are beneficial to humanity. Some of these – the celestial beings – have never experienced existence on Earth, while other advanced beings have previously gone through the gamut of lives on Earth or other planetary systems and have moved into higher dimensions.

Now let us consider the two lower dimensions – first, the one immediately below you.

The entities which exist here are of a form which most of you would consider totally grotesque and repulsive – quite literally the stuff of nightmares. In their existence, emotions are totally unknown, as is the power of conscious thought; if you consider the lowest life-form of those which have ever existed on earth, you are looking at creatures which are considerably more highly-evolved than anything which exists in the second dimension.

Most humans have had dreams while asleep, and – as we have said – during dreams the conscious mind is stilled, which allows the mental and emotional bodies to travel and enter other dimensions, which may be either above or below your third dimension. Now when seeing the entities in the lower dimensions – in your terms, having nightmares – the dreamers have often been terrified by what they have experienced – and so have introduced emotion into that dimension, where it did not exist before. This had an effect on those entities native to that dimension – which found out that it was pleasant and so were attracted to it.

In this context it may be useful to think of what drug-users sometimes describe about the state that they get into when having a "good trip" in a higher dimension. They may see lights, colours, hear beautiful music and generally have a pleasant experience. That was – and still is – the effect that emotions of most sorts have on a lower entity.

But some of those entities clung to the emotional bodies of the people when they returned to the Earth – when they woke up – and here they found a true heaven, where they were surrounded on all sides by a complete range of emotions. Some of these they found pleasant – the ones which were nearest to their own dimension, the lower emotions of Fear, Hatred and Anger – while others were less pleasant, the higher emotions of Kindness, Sympathy, Compassion, and above all, Love, which was farthest away.

To give a simple analogy in human terms of why this was so, all human being are attracted towards light, and darkness is feared and associated with all kinds of unpleasant threats and activities. However, when sunlight becomes too bright it is blinding, and so you tend to use ways of stepping it down, by the use of sunglasses, for instance, and in many cases you prefer to stay in the shade rather than in the full glare of the sun.

And this is exactly the same for those second dimensional entities who come into your world – they shun the vibrations produced by the higher emotions. But by using a human word such as *shun* we are attributing a human sense to an entity which does not have it. The entities cannot think, so they do not deliberately decide to avoid such emotions. Their reaction when brought into the presence of a vibration which is too high is totally involuntary and automatic, they just draw away – in the same way that certain primitive life-forms in your world draw away from conditions which they sense as harmful.

Once having been brought through into your third dimension, the entities had no way of returning to their natural home, so they stayed, and now exist in very large numbers throughout your world. They congregate anywhere where there are crowds of people, as the more that people are together the more there is a likelihood of lower emotions surfacing. For instance, in most major sporting events, it is inevitable that there will be many spectators who are delighted with the outcome of the game, match or contest, but almost certainly there will be as many that will be disappointed. And the entities there will have a rich feast in attaching themselves to those people who are suffering the disappointment.

When an entity attaches itself to human beings in order to feed off the negative emotion which they are experiencing, it also brings its own natural energy with it – and the human beings, through their auras will sense that energy as being dull, numbing and depleting, for as long as the entity stays with them.

Human beings who have entities attached to them over a period of time do not necessarily know it – most people are totally unaware of even the *existence* of entities – so they can have no idea at all of what is affecting them. But they are certainly conscious of the effects which they feel, a dull heaviness, a dragging down, a lethargy and unwillingness to take any positive action. The general term which you use for this condition is *depression*. Once people have an entity attached, they will start to feel depressed, and the more depressed they feel the more emotion the entity has to feed on, so the longer it will stay. This is why depression is often seen as a self-generating illness.

We have spoken about only one of the range of negative human emotions – that of disappointment – but the same principle will apply for all the others. Sorrow is the most obvious one, and there can be few people who have not experienced the dull heaviness which exists around funeral ceremonies. But it is an interesting phenomenon that after the actual ceremony in the cemetery or crematorium, the general mood of the mourners lightens. Of course, in many societies it is the custom to have a wake after the ceremony, so it is quite natural that as the alcohol flows people's spirits will be lifted, but that is not the only reason why it happens. It can happen even in a teetotal gathering, for this reason:

In general, people do not like to feel sad. Of course, there will always be some extreme cases of those who live in such a state of negativity that they *expect* their lives to be full of trouble and problems and so, paradoxically, are really only content when they are surrounded by grief, sorrow and disappointment – but fortunately such pitiable creatures are in a tiny minority.

Apart from such rare cases, most people are uncomfortable with the emotion of sorrow, and tend to avoid it whenever possible: it takes a very special kind of person to be able to deliberately contact and try to comfort someone who has been bereaved. But once the actual funeral ceremony has been held, most people will wish to turn the conversation away from the dear departed or the implications of his/ her death for the remaining family onto more general topics. And when someone's mind turns to other topics, the emotions will follow it, and so deprive the entities which are present of the very thing which attracts them – negative emotions.

Once one person has taken a lead, it seems to have an almost exponential effect on the whole gathering, and often there is a perceivable change in the general atmosphere within minutes. Even those immediately affected by the death – widow, widower or children – often feel the change as well. Of course, in many societies, they are expected to put on a brave face, and do their actual grieving in private, so they also welcome the opportunity to lighten the conversation. The final result is that there is nothing left for the entities to feed on, and they leave.

So all negative emotions will attract the attention of negative entities – which is a very good reason for always trying to "look on the bright side of life," as one of your songs says. You have been told already by others that a negative mental attitude is harmful to you, and this is the main reason why. Negativity attracts second dimensional entities, which feed on the emotions felt and depress the person concerned even more, which creates more negativity – and a vicious spiral downwards is created.

But if *you* are affected, how can you stop the downward trend, once it has started? It is not enough to say "Be more positive!" as that is very difficult if your mood has sunk down very far. So you need to have some way of breaking the mental and emotional pattern which is causing the problem. There are different ways of doing this, some of which are more effective than others. Some of them will also be more appropriate than others, depending on your circumstances – just choose which one feels right for you.

All of the methods are variations on the theme of neutralising the negativity, which will mean that the entity or entities attached to the person will simply leave, for lack of nourishment. One method is to start associating with others who are themselves always positive. You have been told about the aura which is around each person, and how it can interact with the auras of others. By an exchange of energy between auras, each person is affected, so if you are with people who are very positive some of that positivity will rub off onto you, and benefit you.

But some of *your* negativity will also rub off onto *them* so they will be less likely to *want* to associate with you. So how do you get round that problem? Well, some people have a vocation for helping others, either in a paid capacity, such as ministers of religion, psychotherapists or counsellors, or in a personal and voluntary capacity – you would call these people *agony aunts*. Such people will usually know how to protect themselves against detrimental influences, and we shall be speaking more about protection later.

A more unusual form of self-help is to consult a psychic who specialises in clearing out harmful entities. This is usually necessary only in extreme cases, where more harmful types of entities – from the first dimension – are concerned, and these entities are often attached not only to an individual but also to a place. This kind of help is usually known as exorcism, space-clearing or Feng Shui.

A simpler form of psychic help is to have spiritual healing. This is done in different ways in various therapies or faiths, sometimes by the laying-on of hands, sometimes absently through concentration or prayer, but all have the same basic intention – to introduce the power of Love into the person's condition. We said earlier that entities cannot bear the vibrations of the higher emotions, and so when they come into contact with Love – which has the highest vibration of all, that of the particles of the primary energy of the universe – they immediately remove themselves from the person.

However, what if none of these methods really appeal to you? What if you don't have the means, or the opportunity, to consult a professional, and neither do you have any form of religious or philosophical mindset which would enable you to consult a priest or a psychic? What can you do then?

Well, in this situation you are brought face to face with the source of the problem – which is you! It started with you, you have it – and you are in the final analysis the best person to sort it out. So how can you do it?

17. Affirmations & 1st Dimensional Entities

This is where we need to speak about the subject of Affirmations. An affirmation is a statement about yourself, a very special statement, the purpose of which is to cancel and remove various negative thoughts which you have about yourself or your life. Most human beings have a negative self-image: there are very few who are completely happy with themselves, and even fewer who are happy with the way that their lives are developing.

In your current Western society, there is an obsession with physical beauty, so there are whole industries devoted to the culture of *the body beautiful*, and countless millions of you agonise about being the right size, shape, weight or appearance. Even more of you worry about your real or supposed mental or emotional shortcomings, and what others think of you. Finally, most of you worry about the pattern of your lives, whether you will ever meet the right mate, get the right job, be able to afford the right sort of holiday or lifestyle, and so on. The list of things which can be wrong in your lives is simply endless.

So let us take a simple – and very common – example: the worry about having no friends or social life, which is the primary thing causing you depression. What is the root cause of this worry? It is the fact that, in your heart of hearts, you do not feel that you are worthy of having friends and a good social life, *because you are not good enough*. So what can you do about that?

* * *

Using affirmations to solve the problem, you would make up a list of statements which *directly contradict* what you currently think. The most important thing which you have to do is to negate the emotion of not loving yourself, so you could simply say "I love myself!" One of the foremost lady gurus of positive thinking in your modern age said that the master affirmation was "I love and *approve* of myself" and this is certainly a more-embracing formula than just to say that you love yourself, as it includes not only your appearance but also your habits, qualities, faults and lifestyle. However, the form of words used is not really important – it is the statement itself, and the emotion behind it, which is important.

Author's note: See Further Reading under Louise L. Hay

The channelling continues:

But what if your self-esteem is so low that you cannot even bring yourself to say those three words – "I love myself?" How can you get things started? Well, a simple way of easing yourself into saying the affirmation might be to say "I *like* myself a little more today than I did yesterday." Once you are happy with that, you might progress to saying "I *love* myself a little more today than I did yesterday." Finally, when saying that is no longer difficult you could say the full affirmation.

While saying affirmations, it is a very good habit to look into a mirror. Look into your eyes, and say the affirmation. The eyes have been called the mirrors of the soul, and certainly when someone looks directly into your eyes and tells you something, you are more likely to accept what they say than if they are not looking at you. So by looking into your own eyes, you are subconsciously more able to accept what is being said. However, we do not mean to imply that it will be an easy thing to convince yourself of this new situation. After all, you may have lived for most of your life believing that you were *not* worthy of love, and so for anyone to start saying that you *are* will take a lot of swallowing.

It has been said, only partly in joke, that when you start to say affirmations, looking into your own eyes in a mirror and saying that you love yourself, your eyes will look back at you and say "You don't!" – so you will almost certainly find that it takes time before you start to accept the process of doing it. The reason for this is that initially your subconscious mind will just refuse to believe what you are saying. While you are saying the words your conscious mind will be telling you that it is all a load of rubbish, and that it cannot do any good at all, or make any change in you or your life. And this is where your will and determination comes into action. If you really *want* to change the reality of your situation you will persevere in your affirmations. It is a good idea to do them every time that you go to the bathroom, so that while you are washing your hands you say the affirmation a dozen or so times. If you do this, after only a short time you will just accept the action as part of a routine, and once you have got to that stage there will be no more *conscious* opposition to doing it.

But what about the *subconscious* opposition, which is far more deep-seated and far less easy to eradicate? Well, if you understand that what you are really doing is self-hypnosis, then over a period of time the affirmation will sink into your subconscious and replace the ideas about yourself which already exist there. Do not expect the process to be quick and easy: it took a lot of negative conditioning to get you to this state, and it will take a lot to undo the harm – but undo it you will.

One thing that will help you in your resolve is to look for signs that your life is changing. Usually, when a person starts a conscious process of trying to change their personal reality some small positive thing happens in their life – almost a sign that he or she is on the right path at last. If you are aware of this it will give you a little boost in your efforts to solve the basic problem.

So how does all this help you to get rid of an entity which is feeding on your negative emotions? Quite simply, the less negative emotions which you have about yourself, the less reason there is for the entity to stay, and even the *repetition* of positive affirmations is enough to start to neutralise the negativity in someone's aura. Many religious organisations have taught for centuries the value of repeatedly saying mantras in order to induce positive conditions around the devotees, and what you are doing with affirmations is only a more personal example of this. We shall say more about the power inherent in words at a later stage.

But success breeds success, and once you have got over your initial dislike of yourself, you can progress to other more complicated matters, having a better job, more friends, a better social life, or whatever your immediate pre-occupations are. So make up an affirmation for each one in turn, such as "I *have* a good job," "I *have* a lot of friends" or "I *have* a good social life." Once more, the form of words does not matter very much – the simpler the statement the more effective it is likely to be, as you can put a certain amount of emphasis into your tone, stressing the word "*have*."

Two final things about affirmations: when you say one, always make sure that the affirmation says that you *have* what you want. Never say that you *will have* it, or you will put the achieving of your wish *permanently* in the future. You will always be saying "I will have it" – i.e. in the future – and it will never come into your present reality.

The other thing that you should avoid is saying any affirmation which includes a negative word. For instance, if you are currently in a bad relationship and your affirmation is "I am not in a bad relationship," your subconscious will pick up the words *not* and *bad*, both of which are negative words, and will act on them. Now in some languages, double negatives cancel each other out, but in others, a double negative reinforces the negativity – and that is what happens with affirmations. So make sure that your affirmations contain no negative words at all.

As a simple example of this, just imagine that you have bad health, and you want to change the situation. If you say, "I have not got bad health" you have a double negative, which will reinforce the idea of you having bad health – and make you worse than before. However, if you say, "I *have* good health" then the affirmation can only be positive.

We have spoken about the entities which are naturally at home in the second dimension, and we have shown how all of these, when attached to a human being, can be harmful, because of their heavy and deadening effect on the emotional body. Now we must turn to the lowest dimension, the first, where the entities are far more harmful and can in many cases be totally devastating.

* * *

Let us first of all consider what the first dimension is: it is the basic dimension on which all others are built, so it may be considered to be without any recognisable form of intelligence when viewed from a human perspective. We said that the entities in the second dimension were without the power of thought, although even they had the ability to sense emotions as pleasant and desirable. But most of the energies in the first dimension have not even that limited capability, despite being formed out of the same particles of intelligent energy as the remainder of Creation.

But the first dimension is also the direct opposite – and so balances – the highest dimension of Creation, the one next to the pure energy of the source. So, if we consider that dimension as the highest expression of purity in Creation, then the first dimension must be the exact opposite to it; if we can coin a phrase, it must be "absolute impurity."

These two attributes of the first dimension give a clue to the kinds of entity which inhabits it, and the first two kinds of entity are both *principles*, rather than anything more describable in human terms. Of these, the first are *elemental* principles, and the entities themselves are usually referred to as *elementals*. They are the principles of elements, the most common of which are known to you as Fire, Air, Water and Earth.

Although you are very familiar with the uses of all of these elements in your daily life, you have only a very limited idea of what each means when expressed on an elemental level. Perhaps if we tell you that the planet herself only touches on the fringes of the energies concerned when manifesting some of her more violent phenomena, that fact may give you food for thought. Consider, for instance, the heat which exists at the core of the earth, which is occasionally seen – in a much modified form – when spewing out in a volcanic eruption. Think of the immense power of a tsunami, or the force of a major hurricane, or the energy of a gigantic earthquake, off the scale of your current measuring instruments, which might be felt on the other side of the world. All of these are examples of elemental power as manifest in your world – and all of them are completely outside the power of human beings to control.

We can say that, with one exception, the elemental forces mentioned cannot be either invoked or controlled, and although your scientists are now inventing some very ingenious devices to harness a very small part of the energy within those four elements, they are really only touching the fringes of the potential energy in each. But there is one way in which science has managed to tap deeper into the energy of one of the elements, and that is in the use of nuclear power, which uses some of the enormous energy of the element of fire.

This is a development which has been of great concern to many of the civilisations on planets in other star systems in your galaxy, as you are running the risks of repeating the errors of previous great civilisations in your world, some of which you know through legends, but most of which are completely unknown to you. You have a very limited view of the history of your species on your planet, and have the strange idea that you are the most advanced of the intelligent life-forms which have ever existed there.

Yet we have to tell you that there have been many other advanced civilisations before you, all of which were swept away by natural disasters, by war, disease and – in at least one era - by nuclear annihilation. If you look in the middle of one of your most inhospitable deserts you will find vast areas of material which cannot be produced naturally, but only by the immense heat of silicon fusing in a nuclear explosion. Those are the last vestiges of that long-forgotten civilisation. If you believe that traces of an ancient highly-developed civilisation would be impossible to eradicate so completely, just consider what would be left of your own civilisation if it were suddenly wiped out today. What would remain in 1,000 years, 10,000 years, 50,000 years? Even your greatest artifact, the carving-out of a mountain into a giant sculpture, would be hardly recognisable after the ceaseless erosion of 100,000 years by the forces of Nature. And when we mention forgotten great civilisations, we are talking about much longer time-spans than that.

Humanity was not *intended* to master nuclear technology until your race was so advanced that there was no possibility of it being used for offensive purposes against others – and by *others* we mean others who currently inhabit your own planet or others within your galaxy. Obviously the prospect of humanity reaching that state of spiritual awareness in the foreseeable future is – to put it mildly – rather remote.

So the elemental entities which we have discussed exist in the first dimension. But what are the other entities which also exist there?

* * *

We now refer to the second group of entities, what we have called the principles of *absolute impurity*. These, like the elementals which we have discussed, are totally without any form of intelligence and so incapable of any directed application, so in essence they are not capable of affecting your human lives at all *without application of external forces*. But note that we have emphasised that last phrase, for you yourselves are very capable of applying the external forces in order to activate those energies.

So what are we talking about when we mention the principles of *absolute impurity*? In short, everything which is the opposite of the higher emotions, everything which impels human beings to harm either themselves, other human beings or other life-forms on the planet. Various sacred texts of different religions warn against these principles in one way or another, and one of your great religions has even codified what it considers the most damaging and has labelled them as "the seven deadly sins." We would make no detailed comment on their classification, but say only that there are many more than seven, and any classification must by nature be highly subjective, according to the religious fervour of a particular day and age. There has been so much written over the centuries about these sins that we do not think it of any value to comment on them here.

* * *

One of the ways that may be used to help those who have entities attached to them is to resort to Spiritual Healing. This is practiced in many societies, and in many ways. Sometimes it is done through ritual and ceremony, sometimes not. It may involve the invocation of a high level spiritual being such a god, saint or angel, or it may involve the healers putting themselves in a state where the healing energy may flow through them without interruption. However, in every case the object is to direct energy – the energy of the primal particles which makes up the created universe – to neutralise the psychic source of the problem within the human being. Then, once that psychic source is totally neutralised, the physical symptoms can no longer exist – and the person is healed.

The same method is used when persons have been attacked by a psychic entity – for instance, having had hatred directed at them – but in this case the darkness which surrounds the entity has to be overcome by the light of the particles which are directed at it. Once more, there are many ways in which this is done, and when a formal ritual is used it is normally known as exorcism. Yet all these ways use essentially the same energy – although that might be hotly disputed by the more fanatical members of some of your religions!

Once the entity has been overcome by the superior force of Love – the primary particles of energy – then it can be sent back to the first dimension, where it belongs, and there it will remain, unless – or rather until – it is once more activated when another misguided human being directs hatred against another victim.

Of course, from the high ground of your modern world, you may dismiss with contempt the idea of a person being possessed by an evil spirit, although you have been told of the existence of such beings countless times throughout your history. Your medical scientists who specialise in the study of psychology have always tried to find logical factual reasons for mental illness, and in many cases the more advanced thinkers have come very near to the truth – for instance when they put forward ideas about universal consciousness or group souls – but they have always shied away from theories about psychic possession. Perhaps, in the most obvious cases, where patients complain of hearing voices which tell them to carry out all sorts of criminal acts, it might be of value to call in a psychic who specialises in exorcism when all other traditional forms of therapy have been tried and failed.

Since we have touched on psychotherapy, it may be a very fruitful avenue for those who have patients with schizophrenia to consider a possible reason why they have problems: they are living in two worlds at the same time, and cannot distinguish between the two. We have already outlined the process which is used for a soul to be incarnated into a human body. And you have been told that the last thing which has to be done during pregnancy is that the interface, which will join the emotional body to the physical foetus, has to be created and attached – a very lengthy and delicate operation which takes up to three months to achieve. Finally, when the interface is fully integrated with the foetus, the child is born.

Now for much of the child's early life, and certainly for the first two years, it may still remember its previous existence in the fourth dimension, from which it came, and this is why so many parents tell stories of their children seeing non-material things. Some of them have spirit friends with whom they play, some have psychic animals as pets, and others can see – and converse with – people who have died or are, if you prefer to use the term, *ghosts*. The wise parent, faced with this situation, will gently tell the child that what he or she is seeing is living in another world, and not in the normal everyday world, so that the child is introduced to the idea that there are two worlds, physical and non-physical, and can start to distinguish between them.

In time, of course, most children lose the ability to see non-physical things, as they become more and more immersed in the everyday world of a human being, although some retain this ability into adult life. Many children have their innate ability stamped out of them by parents who simply ridicule what they are seeing, so that they quickly learn not to talk about it, and eventually in many cases become afraid of it. However, there are some who are so psychic that they continually *see* beings in another dimension, with their psychic eye at the same time that they see their surroundings in the physical world with their ordinary eyes. They then have the problem that they are continually told that what they are seeing psychically is just caused by their imagination, and does not really exist, which sets up considerable mental turmoil.

Now the original psychic cause of the problem of schizophrenia is that in the final stages of pregnancy, the interface between the emotional body and the foetus was not completely attached to the foetus, so the baby *did not totally enter into the experience of life as a human being.* In psychic terms, it never became fully grounded.

Every human being, from time to time, has the experience of not being grounded: if your brain is not actively processing the information which you are receiving so that you can carry on your normal life, you are not grounded. There are many ways in which this can show itself – you have derogatory terms such as "not in this world," "airy-fairy," or "walking in the clouds" to describe someone who is not consciously taking note of what is going on round him. But even something as mundane as tripping up over something which you did not see is an indication that – at least temporarily – you are not grounded. But when someone suffers from schizophrenia they are experiencing this all the time.

So how can you help people to ground themselves? Note that we have not said, "How can you ground them?" because that is not possible: they have to do it for themselves. Well, there are many ways, most of which involve some sort of mental imagery. One which does not – and which is actually the simplest of all – is just to say to themselves three times "Ground! Ground! Ground!" (This is useful when you have a momentary loss of concentration, as in our example of tripping up: you are just giving yourself a mild ticking-off and telling yourself to be more careful.)

There are techniques involving visualisation which usually ask the person to imagine that roots are growing from their body and going down into the earth, either through the soles of their feet or from the base of their spine. One such exercise involves sitting the person comfortably in a chair and then telling them to imagine the coccyx – the vestigial human tail – growing and extending down to the earth. Then, once it touches the earth, it takes root, grows bigger and thicker until the person feels that he or she is attached to the earth by a huge tree-trunk. The person is told to concentrate on this experience, noting what it feels like, and is told to remember that feeling when the exercise is finished, so that he or she can always go back to that state at any time in the future. Then, after a suitable time, he or she is gently brought back and told that they are always connected to the earth, and can do the same exercise at will whenever necessary.

Perhaps there are some brave psychotherapists in your world who might be prepared to explore this idea with some of their more difficult cases and see if there is some truth in what we have said!

* * *

18. "The Fall," Guides and Angels

We now refer to the final – and most destructive – of the types of entity which inhabit the first dimension, and to explain these we have to resort to talking about the traditions of many of your religions, as there is no comparable material within your scientific knowledge. In most of your religious material there are stories of evil beings which, in some way or another – the details vary according to the religion – "fell from grace" and separated themselves from the mainstream of Creation. We will explain the origin of these differing legends and, more importantly, the way in which you are all affected during your current human existence.

You have heard how the Big Bang brought into being a concentration of different densities of particles, of different kinds and at different vibrational frequencies, some of which you can recognise and some which you can not, and how this has evolved into your current universe. You have heard how, in your own small portion of the universe, souls experience third dimensional existence, with all its pleasures but then, due to the Law of Cause and Effect, become enmeshed and trapped within the human condition. They then alternate between third and fourth dimensional existence – what one of your religions calls the Wheel of Rebirth – until they eventually free themselves and can move on to other experiences in the fifth dimension.

But when we have spoken about souls we have mentioned only a tiny proportion of the life-forms which exist in the whole of Creation: there are very many others, most of which are totally unknown to you – although some of your more imaginative writers of science fiction have been able to describe these life-forms in other galaxies. In many of your human cultures you have stories of other kinds of being – spiritual beings – which are seen from time to time by those who have special psychic gifts, but which do not usually interact with human beings.

You have been told that souls have a gradual evolution in consciousness through the dimensions, and that movement from each dimension to the next one can be achieved only when everything in that lower dimension has been learnt. But we have not yet spoken of what happens in the ultimate transition, where everything has been learnt, and everything has been experienced.

The answer to that enigma is that the soul is finally dissolved into its constituent particles, the primal particles of energy, and those particles are then assimilated into the universal ocean of particles which was the initial home from which they came. All thoughts of separate identity are realised to be mere illusions, and each particle which was part of a soul now knows that it is part of everything that is. There is no separation, for there is no differentiation – everything is total peace, harmony, calm – and Love.

This is a concept which no human being can understand, as it is beyond human experience. One of your religions talks of the ultimate state as being Nirvana, but most describe it in human terms, as being light, peace, comfort, warmth and happiness – which is as far as you can get in your imagination.

* * *

Now the same thing applies to every other life-form in Creation. Although each one has its separate characteristics and qualities, each can only exist as long as its environment exists – and the conditions for the creation and extinction of different environments are not the same. However, all are subject to a continual movement, a continual flow or change – nothing is ever the same for any two consecutive periods of time. We have to use a human term here in order to give some basis for understanding: in truth, time does not exist: past, present and future all co-exist in the ultimate reality.

At one moment very early in the evolution of your universe, long before your galaxy had been formed, one of an order of celestial beings had come to the end of its own evolution. This entity had experienced everything that it was intended to experience, within the framework of the created blueprint of its order, and was about to become assimilated once more into the initial state of primary particles. However, it became affected by the impurity of Pride – which is, incidentally, one of the most devastating of all impurities. This is because it works in a most insidious way, and can sneakily creep up on even the most high-minded individuals, without them knowing consciously what is happening to them. The entity realised that it was at the apex of experience as a separate identity, and that its next movement would be into the overall sea of undifferentiated existence, where it would no longer have a separate personality. The contamination of the impurity caused it to rebel against its own natural progression, and to refuse to graduate, and try to show that it was more powerful than the system in which it was existing.

In order to understand the result of this, we will give you a human analogy: just imagine that you are swimming in a river, and find that you are being drawn, at an increasing speed, towards a distant waterfall. What do you do? Well, you *could* try to swim against the current, but after a time you would find out that the force of the water was too strong for your continued resistance, and you would start to tire and be swept downstream once more. What can you now do to avoid your eventual demise? The only thing that you *could* do to escape would be to swim to the side of the river and get out of the flow of water, and so this is presumably what you would attempt to do.

So this is exactly what this exalted entity did: it got out of the Flow, which in its case meant moving down to the dimension below. The human analogy for this would be returning to a point further upstream where the force of the current was not so great. And of course, this action reinforced its belief in its own importance and power – it had beaten the system – leading to more contamination by the impurity of Pride. Not only that, but it persuaded other celestial beings of the same order, which had reached only this lower dimension in their own evolution, that they could follow its example and opt out of the system.

The fact that it had acquired a following further inflated its own feeling of importance, and drew in more impurity. But now the down-side of being clothed with impurity began to show itself, as it became uncomfortable in the dimension where it was, and so retired to the next lower one.

* * *

Over the following aeons of time, the process was repeated. The entity compared itself, its abilities and power, with the entities which were inhabitants of the dimension in which it was, and gloried in its own supremacy, thereby drawing in more Pride. It was able to persuade many of those entities of its own importance, and draw them to accept itself as their leader, and so its band of followers continually grew. But once more, as it became more tainted with the impurity, the dimension in which it was currently existing began to feel less hospitable, as the impurity was not naturally found there. So the entity began to feel uncomfortable, and retired down to the next dimension below, taking its followers with it.

At one particular time, it had the idea of returning to a higher dimension to boast of the numbers of its followers, but found that it was unable to reach that dimension. It had effectively barred itself from returning. This is another example – a rather extreme one, but still an example – of the application of the overall law of which we have spoken so often, the Law of Cause and Effect, and it shows that it operates on all levels of Creation, even on the highest.

Some of your religions paint lurid pictures about the entity incurring the displeasure of a higher entity – or in your terms, a god – who banished it from the celestial realms where it had lived. No such single event happened: everything happened over a long period of time, and by its own actions the entity effectively sealed the doors behind it as it sank down through the dimensions.

Now at this juncture, the entity began to be affected by another impurity, that of Envy, as it started to envy those beings which it had met on its journey down through the dimensions; it envied them because, although it still had enormous power, it could no longer exist in the same place as them: in fact, in a very real sense, they were now more advanced than it was. But the accumulation of Envy soon brought its own punishment, as it found itself unable to remain in the dimension where it was, and was forced to retreat to a lower dimension again – after which the door was closed once more.

Up to this time the entity had generally accepted the overall system of Creation, but as it sank lower it realised what a dreadful punishment it had brought on itself by opting-out of that system, and so another devastating impurity began to affect it – the impurity of Hatred. It hated the system, it hated all who were in the system, and it hated all those who were, by their own efforts, moving up through the system to higher dimensions – not realising that by expressing Hatred it was harming itself even more. And in due course the inevitable effect happened – it was no longer able to stay in that current dimension and had to move down once more.

So it was that in the course of time – an unimaginable length of time – the entity, with all its followers, arrived at the lowest dimension, where it co-existed with all the impurities of that dimension, and there it stayed, without possibility of further advancement. It stayed there for aeons of time, stuck in the foetid conditions of the first dimension until one day, in a tiny third-dimensional planet in a remote corner of a galaxy far from the centre of one of the universes, something interesting happened: your species had evolved to a state where it was capable of independent thought. And with independent thought came the ability to express emotions in a more directed way than had been possible before the emotional body had evolved out of the original simple basic instincts of lower life-forms.

It was now possible for human beings not only to *experience* a wide range of feelings in respect of others, but also to *express* those feelings in rational thoughts, many of which drew on basic impurities such as Hatred and led to actions against others. And by drawing on those impurities, they opened up a portal for entities in the first dimension to enter directly into the third – and enter they did! They soon found out that human beings were very easy to influence, and because the human species was very young, for a time the harmful entities were able to wreak havoc and delay the evolution of the species.

Why did they do this? We have said that the original entity was consumed by Hatred of everything and everyone, and this soon rubbed off on its followers, so that when they had the opportunity of expressing that Hatred against relatively defenceless human beings, they revelled in the chaos which they could cause.

The way that they wreaked havoc was by influencing human beings not only to act against each other – through the impurities of Lust,

Hatred and Greed – but also to do things which were not for their own well-being. As the impurity of Gluttony was fostered and encouraged, the person would adversely affect their own physical health, and also Idleness affected their physical and mental health. But the impurity which is arguably the most disruptive in daily human life – and which, strangely enough, you do not consider as an impurity at all – is that of Fear.

It is an interesting fact that this impurity of Fear is still one of the most devastating in your lives today. You fear everything and everyone, both on a personal level – about your own health and welfare – a social level – what others think of you, or whether they will take your job – a national level – how different political parties would change your lives – and on an international level – whether or not other nations will attack you, either directly or indirectly, by warfare or economic and financial power. And of course many of your religions, which *should* be concerned for your welfare, terrorise you by instilling in you a fear of what will happen unless you do things which please ...... (insert the name of the appropriate Supreme Being)

But of course, apart from the actions of harmful entities, the basic law – Cause and Effect – was operating in the lives of the new humans also, and after many lives whatever they had done to others, what we may call their Karmic debt, began to restrict their original freedom of action: they had predestined themselves to having certain unpleasant experiences, and so their spiritual education could start. In some philosophies you refer to the Earth as being a schoolhouse of learning, and this is in fact correct. As you go through a succession of lives, and have to repay more and more Karmic debts, you start to wonder why things happen as they do, and eventually wonder what is the point of it all. It is then that you start to make a great leap forward on your evolutionary journey towards the next dimension – and eventually to higher ones still.

But while the entities were doing their utmost to hold back the evolution of the human species, another factor was operating for good in the lives of the new human beings. The original blueprints for the species had been laid down ages before by the advanced beings which were responsible for creating the new life-form, and it was not to their advantage to have all their work nullified by the interference of the fallen entities. So they were working very hard to try to influence human beings *against* doing anything for which they would be punished in a future life. However, despite all their efforts, there was little that they could do unless – or more correctly *until* – the human beings were ready to listen. And that would be many hundreds of lives into the future.

And so we come up to your modern day: the harmful entities are still working to hold you back, the beneficial beings are still working to try to help you progress, and you are in the middle of these two forces. Philosophically you call it the eternal struggle between Good and Evil, but that is not strictly speaking correct. The two forces are not directly opposed to each other, for if they were the forces of Good, using the power of Love, the primal energy of Creation, would easily overcome the others. To be more exact, the two forces are vying with each other to control the hearts and minds of you and your fellow human beings – and *you* always have the choice of which way you will go: you have Free-will.

If you are reading these words, there is a good chance that you are already fairly well advanced in your spiritual journey through the third dimension – regardless of whether you believe that what we are saying is true or false: it is the fact of having an enquiring mind that is the most important thing – and it is that enquiring mind which will eventually lead you to the Truth. Do not blindly accept that everything which we have said is absolute Truth – although it *is*, from our point of view. But by the same token, do not dismiss everything as being totally wrong. Rather, use what we have said as a base from which you can evaluate your own current views about the nature of Reality. If you are at one or the other extreme of philosophical thinking – the scientific or the religious – we realise that you will dismiss most of this book as "Rubbish." But have we said anything which will advance your own knowledge or views, explain some of the anomalies which perplex you, or make you less intolerant of the beliefs of those at the other extreme? You are eventually responsible for your own evolution – no one can do it for you – and by having a yardstick against which to examine your views you are furthering that evolution. Once more, it will be in the examination that you will move forward.

* * *

Each of you has at least one discarnate being – some have many more – who is attached to you for the whole of your life, who has taken on the voluntary job of guiding you through your life and helping you to achieve your objectives. All of these beings will have reached the fifth dimension, some will have reached that where we are, while a few will have progressed much further.

Two questions are appropriate here: first, why should anyone volunteer to take on the job of looking after someone else for a whole lifetime, and what do they get out of it? And second, what decides from which level a being comes down to provide such a service?

The answers to both questions lie, in a way, in the last word of that paragraph – Service. The whole of Creation came about as an outburst of Love, and the highest method of expressing Love is by rendering service to others. You find this in many ways in your earthly life, where the concept of Service exists in many of your organisations, public or private, and the lives of many individuals are totally taken up with service of some kind or other to the needs of others. So as a being goes up through the different dimensions, the idea of service to Humanity – the wish to help individuals and the whole human race to rise above the relative drabness and squalor of human existence into the splendour of the higher dimensions, becomes very important.

So there are innumerable beings from higher dimensions who are only too willing to take on the care and guidance of a human being through the whole of his/ her lifetime, however long it may be. And what if the lifetime lasts for a hundred years or more? Well, time is a facet of existence only on your Earth – the word has no meaning whatsoever in the higher dimensions. Some of you will be familiar with the poetic words which say that "A thousand ages .... are like an evening gone" – so a term of service of a mere hundred years or so is like the blinking of an eyelid.

As far as the second question is concerned, all of you were at different levels of understanding when you came into your present incarnation on Earth, and so you needed helpers and guides who were themselves at different levels. Let us take the simple analogy of children going to school. All enter by the same door, but then they make their way to different classrooms, where they have different teachers. Those who are starting at the school will have teachers specialising in early-year teaching, while those who are sitting national examinations will have teachers capable of teaching at that level. So, the level of teaching will depend on the level which the pupil has reached – and so it is with all human beings, as they make their way through the hundreds of lives which they will have in a physical body. The more that they understand about the true meaning of life and the connection between your own world and the entirety of Creation, the higher the dimension from which their teachers will come.

The highest non-physical beings who can be called on to help humanity are those who are grouped under the general heading of Angelic Beings. We have mentioned these previously, so will merely say briefly that there are several different orders of such beings, and there is much information about them in the writings of many of your religions. Some of you will be familiar with names such as Archangels, Cherubim and Seraphim, but the actual names of the different orders are unimportant. The function of all of these beings is to provide Service throughout the different dimensions to all life-forms in all universes, and they are capable of working in all dimensions up to the final one, where all manifestation is dissolved into the final state of undifferentiated energy.

We should say that your idea of angelic beings as having human form, with the addition of wings, is a totally erroneous one, and comes from the fact that in most cases you are completely unable to understand the concept of discarnate beings, and so have to personalise everything. Angelic beings are in fact composed of energy expressed as light, at different intensities, and so the structure and organisation of their different orders bears no resemblance whatsoever to anything which exists in human experience.

So we have pointed out that, despite the fact that you are all exposed to possible attacks from harmful entities, you have a great number of beneficial beings on whom you can call to help you in your pathway through your many lives. However, the most interesting thing is that there is a great difference between your reaction with the harmful entities and with those beneficial *light-beings*. The harmful entities will take every opportunity to attach themselves to you, and to feast on the negative emotions which are so part of your human lives, whereas the light-beings will come to your aid *only when they are invited in*. They are not allowed to directly influence you unless you *want* to be influenced, as to do so would totally neutralise the life lessons which you have come to the Earth to learn.

Now this leads to a very interesting situation, in which human beings, newly started on their journey through earthly incarnations, will normally be affected only by harmful entities. They will be experiencing the new delights of existence in a physical body, without having any knowledge or experience of any of the higher beings available to help them, and so will be rapidly dragged down to experiencing all of the impurities of which we have spoken. This, then, will inevitably lead to the negative energies of the actions which they are taking attaching themselves to the subtle bodies, and gluing them together in the way that we have described.

However, after many hundreds of lives of learning what is and is not appropriate behaviour in a human body, (through the eternal law of Cause and Effect), they will start to become aware that there *are* higher beings in existence, and that these beings may be called on to help in various situations, and from then on things will start to change. It will not happen overnight – rather over a period of hundreds of lives – but happen it will. Gradually the balance will shift from living lives which are completely dominated by the depredations of harmful entities to living ones which are largely coloured by the helpful inspiration and actions of light-beings.

* * *

There will never be a life in which the harmful entities are totally absent. As we pointed out earlier, one of the most advanced light-beings in Creation was eventually brought down because it was affected by the impurity of Pride and "fell" – so there is always the possibility of being affected and dragged back down to a situation where lessons have to be re-learnt. However, the more that you are aware of the light-beings the more you will be influenced by them – and *use* them. We emphasise the word use, as so many of you who *do* know about these beings think of them in a purely detached way, much as you think about the moon: it is there, but it doesn't really have much to do with your daily life, so forget it and just carry on with your life.

In fact, light-beings are available for you to use, invoke, call on and invite into your lives. Just try it out for yourself, and see what happens. Start with something totally mundane, like trying to find an article which you have put down somewhere and can no longer find. Ask whoever you wish to inspire you to help you to remember where it is, and see what transpires. Then, if it works on that level, try something else with which you need help or inspiration. When you start to do this on a regular basis, you will be amazed at what can happen. There are some who call on light-beings continually, and who swear that they are helped every time that they do, so you could well find that it will help you, too.

* * *

19. Sound and Music

Many centuries ago scientists realised that sound was an audible range of vibrations, and since then your knowledge has expanded to the level where you can now produce machines which locate and measure the distance of unseen objects, or *see* medical anomalies which exist within the human body. But we would dare to tell you that so far you have only scratched the surface of what there is to be learnt about sound, and cannot yet achieve some applications which were known in the ancient world – for instance the use of sound to achieve levitation.

Also, much of the research which has been done by some of your scientists working at the fringe of sound has been either totally ignored or at best treated with the mild disdain of the serious scientist towards others who are considered amateur dabblers in the subject. This attitude is akin to that of those adults who view the antics of their children with tolerance and mild amusement, part of the natural progression towards growing up and ceasing to play games.

We mention only two areas where information which is absolutely vital for the wellbeing of the human race has been largely overlooked. The first is in the series of experiments where *words* have been chanted over a container of water, and then the structure of the molecules of that water have been photographed and analysed. The analysis showed that there was a marked difference in the symmetry and harmony of the different structures *depending on which words had been chanted over the water*. Where words like "Love," "Peace," or "Harmony" had been chanted, the resultant pattern of the structure was beautiful and symmetrical, whereas the exact opposite was found where words like "Hate," "War" – or even the name of some infamous human being in history – resulted in a distorted and ugly pattern.

Author's Note: *See Further Reading under Emoto, Masaru.*

The channelling continues:

This simple experiment proved that words have power to affect inert substances – something which is largely ignored in your modern society – and if this is so in connection with water, how much more will it be true when words are used for or against human beings – who are, incidentally, largely composed of water? Elsewhere, you have been told of the importance of the early years of a child's development, and during those years a great deal of the influence is through the words which are said to the child. Kindness and gentleness, expressed in words, will be highly beneficial, whereas roughness and harsh words will be detrimental.

Another of the areas of research into the use of sound which has been largely ignored by orthodox scientists is in the study of the effects of music on human beings. Studies of the harmonic structure of the works of different great composers showed that they had different effects on the minds of many individuals, and particularly on the minds of children. In one incredible series of experiments, a primary school teacher played different pieces of music to a class of very unruly primary children, and was amazed to find that they produced different effects. In one exceptional instance, works by one particular classical composer brought total and utter harmony to the whole class, and had a continuing effect for a considerable time after the music had stopped.

Author's Note: *See Further Reading under Tomatis, Alfred, and also under Lingerman, Hal. In the specific instance quoted the composer was Mozart.*

The channelling continues:

It has been a practice in religious circles for centuries to use sound, either by using words – as in repeated chanting of prayers or mantras – music – as in the humming or singing of single notes or successions of notes – or by using a combination of words and music – as in the singing of hymns or anthems. The object of all of these practices has been to induce in the individual either a sense of peace or a sense of exhilaration, depending on the context.

Of course, the same methods have been used on many occasions in a political context, for instance to induce in those who took part in the singing or chanting a fervent sense of patriotism, and to rouse them up to fight against their real or perceived enemies. Most of your national anthems fall into this category. Indeed, you have only to look at your information media to see pictures of some political, religious or social demonstration somewhere in your world where the crowd is being roused with fervent and repeated chants so that they start to act against what is seen as injustice – and in many cases fight against the forces of law and order who are seen to be protecting the *status quo*.

It is very difficult to avoid the rush of emotion which is caused by being part of a crowd who are all singing or chanting the same thing, and this does not have to be when the crowd is voicing disapproval. For instance, in one of your traditional annual musical events, the last night of the series of concerts culminates with fervent outpouring of emotion where all present sing a famous patriotic song – and few people hearing it can fail to be moved by this.

* * *

However, the practical use of the series of experiments with sound has been totally ignored by most of your scientists, and certainly by all of your politicians. Sound is a very potent force, and can very easily be used as a tool to change behaviour. To show that this has a universal application, and is not confined to the field of human activity, we would mention the experiment which was done some years ago by one of your farmers – certainly an enthusiastic amateur dabbler – who found out by chance that playing soothing music to his cows while they were being milked resulted in them giving increased yields of milk at every session. The fact was seized on by a local newspaper, reported and even had a mention in the national press. It raised some eyebrows, caused a few laughs – and was then promptly forgotten.

So let us say something about the phenomenon of sound and how it can affect behaviour, not only in human beings but in other life-forms on your planet as well. First, you have to understand that sound is composed of vibrations, and individual notes are the production of vibrations of different frequencies, within a limited range of frequencies which is capable of being sensed by the hearing organs of humans. There are a vast number of frequencies which are capable of affecting the human race, but for the present purposes we will confine ourselves only to those which fall within the audible range.

Each sound which you can hear is processed by the physical parts of your hearing system and conducted to your brain, where it is analysed, in the first place by the emotional body. (We have already mentioned the different subtle bodies which exist within the human being, so we will not repeat that information here.) You will remember that the emotional body is the human equivalent of the much cruder basic instinct of an animal, and the primary analysis of the sound is to establish whether or not it is threatening in any way. If it is felt to be threatening, the information is passed to the mental body, which is then able to decide consciously on a course of action. If no immediate threat is perceived, the sound is simply registered on a sub-conscious level and is accepted.

Now let us talk specifically about the role of music and how it can affect behaviour. It is rarely perceived as a threat when it is heard, although perhaps harassed parents might disagree, when faced with raucous music being played at high volume through some audio apparatus by errant children. In fact, at one time or other most parents will have yelled at children who are playing songs by their favourite group too loudly.

So let us imagine that the music has got through the initial *danger* test and has been accepted. It will now start to react with the emotional body, which is itself tuned into a range of vibrations, and will affect those vibrations in some way or other. Where the music is compatible with the emotional body, it will induce feelings of pleasure, and depending on how intense those feelings are, the fact may or may not be transmitted to the mental body, so that it can be noted down for future reference. Of course, in the opposite case, where the music is not compatible, it will create a feeling of unease, and this may similarly be transmitted and, in extreme circumstances, cause the person to switch the music off.

But what decides whether or not the music is compatible with the vibrations of the emotional body of a given human being? Before answering that we must tell you that all music, of *every* kind, is composed of individual notes and chords – combinations of notes played together. There are mathematical rules which govern the relation of the frequencies of individual notes to each other – what are called the *intervals* between notes – and decide which intervals are harmonious to human hearing and which are not. A harmonious chord is one which contains notes, all of which are compatible with each other, whereas an inharmonious chord is one containing notes which are not. All of this is already known to musicians, but for those of you who are not, playing – together – any three notes which are immediately adjacent to each other on a piano will show you what an inharmonious chord is.

Normally a piece of music will contain chords which are mainly harmonious, but occasionally in the composition, and to produce a specific effect, a chord will consist of notes which are not harmonious – a discord. However, when this happens, the music will usually rapidly return to harmonious chords again. In musical terms, the discord will have been *resolved*.

Finally, we have to tell you that the more inharmonious chords that there are in any piece of music, the more it is likely to jar on the ears of most people who listen to it – there is a limit to how much musical disharmony most people can accept at any one time!

* * *

But, you might object, sounds which are perfectly acceptable to some human beings are intolerable to others, so why is that? Well, we now have to tell you that every human being is different – which you already knew – because each human being *vibrates on a different frequency to every other human being*. This is probably a new concept to many of you, so it needs to be explained more fully.

We have already said that all matter consists of elementary particles, which come together in increasing densities in order to form more and more complex structures, ranging from single atoms up to a complete living being. We also said that as they increase in complexity, the vibrationary rate changes, and becomes lower. We refer you to the section on the formation of a human being and how it was impossible to pass from the high frequency of the primary particles directly into the low frequency of physical flesh, which necessitated the creation of intermediate subtle bodies and their respective interfaces.

Author's note: *See Chapter 5.*

The channelling continues:

So when the final result – the human being – exists it does so as a composite of a whole range of vibrations. It might help to think of all the various elements as being individual musical notes, so that the final product is one complete chord, in which all notes are represented. Musically, when a chord is played, the individual notes all merge together so that for all practical purposes they lose their identity in the overall chord.

But – you might object – why are all human beings different, if the process which has been used in their formation is the same in every case? Once more, we have to refer you back to what has already been explained: we said that on its first excursion into complete existence as a human being – having learnt everything about existence in the animal kingdom – the grouping of particles which would henceforth be known as the human *soul* was free to experience everything within its novel three-dimensional environment, and started to do so. But the only guidance which it had for behaviour came from what it had already experienced in animals, so for many lifetimes it behaved as an animal, while being physically human – this enables you to understand your modern phenomenon of feral gangs of young people who apparently have none of the attributes of character which you consider normal in human behaviour.

But every experience which it had, added something to the overall composite of vibrations which formed its basic being; in our musical analogy, it added a new note to the existing chord. So the composite of vibrations, which had started off by being in harmony, rapidly became distorted. Some experiences added vibrations which were harmonious, but many – initially probably *most* – added those which clashed, and so the overall effect degenerated from its initial purity into the equivalent of total cacophony – a hideous noise.

For those of you who are musical, play a harmonious chord on a piano, and then ask someone who is not musical to add another note to the chord, and then further notes – all randomly selected – and you will see how quickly the original harmony of the chord degenerates into an unbearable din.

However, we said that by the law of Cause and Effect, every action which had been done by the new soul had to be balanced eventually by an equal and opposite action – in vibrational terms, it had to be neutralised by the opposite vibration – and the only way for this to be done was for the soul to experience what it had already done to others. So it was condemned to live out a succession of lives, each of which was designed to teach it what acceptable behaviour is in a human context. Previously, the immersion into a third-dimensional existence had been an interesting and voluntary diversion, but now it had become an inescapable duty.

And so it continued: over a succession of lives the new soul was able to neutralise many of the harmful things which it had done during its initial foray into a physical body, but in doing so it encountered many other challenges, made many *mistakes* – all of which had to be rectified later – and slowly learnt everything which could be learnt in human existence on your planet. Each time that it learnt a new fact, it neutralised the harmful vibration which it had already taken on in a previous life in creating the opposite condition. In our musical analogy, it took out one of the discordant notes from the overall chord. Eventually, after innumerable lives, it learnt that all of the challenges which can be met during human life can be overcome by drawing on the strength and power of its own being, using the force of those particles of primal energy which created it, and – when it had learnt *everything* about the human condition – it decided – and was able – to move on to other experiences in other realms. In our musical analogy, the chord had been restored to perfect harmony.

So this is where you all are, at this moment. You are all on a journey back to the perfection of existence which you had long before you had any knowledge of, or connection to, a life in a physical body. How far are you along the road? You are all at different stages. Some, who have already had many hundreds of lives, are very advanced on your journey, and your vibrational rate is very high; others, with less experiences, are not so advanced, and your rate is lower. But all of you who are reading this information are already well travelled along the road – if you were not, you would not have reached the stage where you would want to learn something of the real meaning of life.

To sum up this little excursion into vibrational rates:

1. every human being has a different rate to everyone else,

2. depending on how far along their own particular journey back to perfection they are.

So we can now go back to where we were in our discussion of the importance of Sound in the lives of all of you.

* * *

We have stated that every experience which you have during your life has the effect of changing your vibrational rate, and this is perfectly true. You can probably understand this quite easily when you consider the major events in your life: if, for instance, you had a major health scare it would certainly bring home to you the value of good health, or if you had the misfortune to be burgled, the devastation which you would feel would probably ensure that you personally would never want to inflict the same misery on someone else, either in this or in any future life.

However, it will be less easy for you to understand that *everything* in your life has some sort of effect on you. It is, after all, part of the experience of being in a human body. Most experiences are so fleeting and everyday that you do not even consciously register them in your mind, but that does not mean to say that they are not registered subconsciously, in your vibrational self – or as you would say if you are of a religious disposition, in your *soul*.

Now some experiences are uplifting, while others are not. Let us consider the analogy of music, which is probably the easiest one to understand: if you hear a beautiful piece of music, you will often feel moved by it, and may well resonate with it so much that you start to sing the song or hum the melody as you are listening to it. Then afterwards, you may well feel, for a short time, a sensation of wellbeing. On the other hand, if you hear music which is full of clashing discords, either played with strident instruments or sung in a strident voice, it is quite likely that you will feel less impressed by it at the end – if indeed you have listened to the end.

The reason for whatever reaction you have lies in the degree of compatibility which the music has with your personal vibrations. Let us imagine that your personal vibrations are the equivalent of a chord played by a full symphony orchestra, and the overall vibration of the music which you hear is a single note on a separate instrument. If the note is played in the same key as that of the overall chord, it will be in harmony, and will meld seamlessly into that overall chord. However, if that note does not appear in the key which is being played, then it will create a discord, which will induce a certain amount of stress into the overall sound. Musicians will easily understand this, and will readily accept that the more foreign that the note is to the overall chord, the more discordant will be the result – and the same principle applies whenever music is being played which clashes with your own personal vibrations.

But let us imagine for a moment that you do not turn the music off, and you allow it to play until the end. The effect of the music will be that your own personal vibrations will have been minutely altered; if it is the first time that you have ever heard that music, or that type of music, your musical knowledge will have been expanded, and you will have learnt something. Whether you have learnt that you like the music, or that you hate it, you will at least *know about it* – and that will have enlarged your experience.

Now one piece of music is hardly going to affect your overall vibrations very much, but as we have said it *will* have a minute effect on those vibrations, adding one more *note* to your overall *chord*. But what will happen if you hear the same, or similar, music once more? Once again, it will have very little effect, just a marginal change in your own vibrations. But if it is repeated incessantly, then very gradually you will notice a change in your overall vibration – in other words, it will change *you*! At least, in practical terms, you will not notice it yourself, but those around you will certainly notice it eventually. Your vibrations will change so that they become more in harmony with what you are listening to. One of your ancient civilisations, which produced many sages over its thousands of years of history, used to point out that a single drop of water would have no effect whatsoever on a stone, yet a succession of drops, over a long period of time, might wear the stone away completely.

In the same manner, a single note – whether harmonious or discordant – would have virtually no effect on the chord being played by a symphony orchestra, but a thousand notes certainly would. If all were harmonious, then they would add to the depth of the chord, without changing its basic structure, whereas if all were discordant they would eventually either completely destroy the original chord or possibly create a new chord, depending on what notes had been added.

We have taken some time to introduce the subject of Sound, for it is of great importance in your lives – of far more importance than you can ever understand – and we have used the analogy of music, because that is something which most of you will understand. But now we will go further, and talk about Sound in a wider context.

Sound was the very first experience of human life which you ever had, for as a foetus in the womb you first became aware of the beating of your mother's heart, and this started the mother-and-child bonding which is so important in the early lives of all children. In your early years, most of what you learned came through speech; first, your parents taught you how to speak, and then taught you using speech. As you grew older, you learnt to distinguish between different tones of voice, recognising some as pleasant and encouraging, and others as reproving and threatening. But even before you were able to speak any words at all, you made sounds in order to tell your parents what you wanted. It is only in recent times that it has been recognised that there is a *universal* language which all babies use in order to convey information to those who are caring for them. There are different sounds which a baby makes when it is hungry, tired, uncomfortable or has wind – and each separate sound *is the same all over the world*, regardless of the culture and of what language is being spoken by adults.

Author's Note: see Further Reading under Kiester, Sally and Edwin.

The channelling continues:

You have been told in great detail how important it is for you to continually express love and acceptance to young children, to give them the best start in life, so we will not dwell on that here, but we will now go further. Earlier, we said that the playing of music had an effect on the overall vibrations of your whole being – what we called your *vibrational body* – but now we tell you that *words themselves* also have an effect on you. We pointed out the study where words had different effects on molecules of water, depending whether the words were beneficial or harmful, so now we can look at how words affect you in general.

We do not need to do anything very complicated in order to demonstrate this: we just need to ask you to read a few words:

LOVE	SYMPATHY	RESPECT	COMFORT
HEALTH	HOPE	PLEASURE	FRIENDSHIP
ACCEPTANCE	LIFE	HAPPINESS	GAIN

What does it make you feel like when you read those words? In most people, whatever their individual status in life, the words will induce a pleasant feeling, possibly evoking memories of past times or of people met and appreciated in the past. All will have their own interpretation of the meaning of each word, but the overall effect on everyone will be an enhancement of the feel-good factor.

Now let us take another set of words, and see how differently you react:

HATRED	INDIFFERENCE	ABUSE	DISCOMFORT
DISEASE	DESPAIR	PAIN	BULLYING
REJECTION	DEATH	SORROW	LOSS

Hasn't your mood changed quickly? Each of the words still evokes memories, but now each memory is negative, reminding you of times or persons which you would rather forget – and in some cases which you have actively *tried* to forget.

There is an interesting difference between this simple exercise and what we were saying about music earlier on. In the case of the music, the original sound was received through your hearing, was assessed by your emotional body to see whether it posed a threat, and was later analysed by your mental body. In the exercise you have just done your eyes read the words and the information passed into your mental body, and drew the appropriate feelings from your emotional body – the opposite process.

* * *

Now what do you think the effect on a young child would be if you continually said words such as *Hate* or *Anger* to him or her? It does not take much reasoning to deduce that it would have a very harmful effect. Yet, much of the language which is used in everyday life has exactly that sort of energy within it. And you are all being attacked by these energies daily, whether you like it or not, for you are hearing *strong language* everywhere, and those energies are continually being absorbed by your emotional body and harming you, whether you realise it or not!

* * *

20. Individual and Mass Ascension

And so we approach the end of the information which we have been channelling through our instrument for the last two years. Why have we been doing this? Because you are approaching the most momentous event that has ever occurred in the history of your planet, and certainly the most important in the history of the human race. We have stated several times that each of you is on a journey through many successive lives towards the full knowledge of what is involved in existing in a physical form on a third-dimensional planet. We have also said that when you have learnt all your lessons and reached the end of your experiences you will end your round of human lives – what is often called the *Wheel of Rebirth* – and will move on to another set of experiences in another planet or dimension.

Now what has happened in the past is that this has taken place on an individual level only, or – on one or two very rare occasions when a whole group of people have reached the end of their respective journeys at the same time – as part of a group. There are several terms for moving into a higher dimensional existence, but the general word which you use is *Ascension*, so that is what we will use. During your round of successive lives to date you have always moved into the fourth dimension, to work and to retrieve information at the end of each life. There you have rested, re-lived your life's activities and made plans for your next incarnation. However, Ascension is the act of moving on to the fifth dimension, and being permanently free of the *need* to live any more restricted lives as human beings on Earth.

So why is this particular period in your history so significant? For two main reasons: the first is that in the past, the normal way in which most human beings have ascended is at the time of the death of the physical body. You have some legends about the ascension of certain rare and gifted individuals who have achieved the transition during their physical lives, but this has happened so few times within Western culture that it has virtually been forgotten.

Author's Note: *There are biblical references to the fact that neither Enoch nor Elijah died in the physical body. Other stories say that Count Racoczy in the 17th Century did not die. Some people believe that the mystifying disappearance of the Mayans can be attributed to a group ascension.*

The channelling continues.

However, this time, not only will there be a mass ascension of those who have come to the end of their round of human lives at approximately the same time, which is unusual enough, but also, that mass ascension will be a translation of the group *while all the individuals are still living.*

But the second reason is of far greater importance, and that is that the planet itself is about to go through its own ascension process. Earlier on we explained that all organisms have their own identity, and their own particular vibration, and this is so not only in organisms which are less complex than a human being, but also in those which are far more complex, at the planetary, stellar and galactic level. Each has its own blueprint of evolution, just as Humanity has a blueprint, and at some time each will move on to the next stage of its own personal destiny.

This has happened many thousands of times throughout the billions of years of the history of Creation, so it is not surprising that the time has come for Earth to move into the next stage of its own journey. However, what *is* amazing is the fact that its own transition, its own ascension, is coinciding with the mass ascension of human beings of which we have spoken. This is something which has never happened before, in the history of Creation and no one, on any level, can do any more than guess at how it will work. This is why at the moment there are beings from all over your universe, and particularly from your own galaxy, which are being attracted into your environment to observe what is happening. It is almost as though there is some great earthly spectacle which has attracted large crowds, who are gathering round to witness what is happening, so that they can return home and say "I was there."

So what will it mean, then, this ascension of the planet and the simultaneous ascension of a large number of its human inhabitants? What does *a large numb*er mean, what percentage of the population? How can you predict who will ascend and who will not? When will everything happen – can you pinpoint the timing? So many questions, and as yet so few answers.

We have to say that we do not *know* exactly what will happen: as we have said, it is the very first time that anything comparable will have happened, so there are no precedents. However, we can draw some conclusions from what has happened before – both in the cases of individual human beings and also where other worlds have ascended in their own time – so let us try to give a reasoned estimate of likely events.

Author's note: *Much of the following information has been well documented, but it is included exactly as it was given.*

The channelling continues:

Let us first look at Ascension on the planetary level. Each planet has its own blueprint, which involves not only the evolution of its physical composition but also the evolution of its life-forms. What has happened in the case of Earth is that the one dominant life-form –

homo sapiens – has had so much effect on the normal functioning of the planet and the interdependence of its different species, that the whole ecosystem is at serious risk of breaking down in many areas. So the first thing that will be done is that the planet will cleanse itself – the Law of Change and Stability in progress – and all current depredations will be stopped. The destruction of the rainforests worldwide will cease, and be reversed, and the massive pollution of large areas of the landmass will be brought to an end. Some of the greatest pollutants of your modern age are plastics, and so all manufactured plastics will be de-materialised into their component elements, and returned to the native environment. There will be massive movements of the Earth's crust, which will result in earthquakes of an intensity never seen before, violent volcanic eruptions and massive tidal waves. Many lands which have for millennia been lost under the sea will re-emerge, and many existing lands will sink beneath the waves.

The climate of many areas of the world will change completely, and many which are now temperate areas will become frozen wastes, while many inhospitable areas will become verdant. The polarities of the North and South Poles will change, and there will be the rapid thawing of the present icecaps, and the re-discovery of legendary long-lost lands. The new atlas of the world will be much different from that of your present age, with some countries having disappeared completely and some having been greatly reduced in size, while others will be enlarged and some completely new land-masses will have appeared.

You have legends about the Golden Age, and as far as the planet is concerned it will rapidly move to a situation where it will once more become a very wonderful, and a very beautiful, place to live in for those who are able to re-colonise it. All existing life-forms, with the sole exception of human beings, will move with the planet and – free of interference from Humanity – will flourish, so that there will be an enormous outburst of creative activity to restore the conditions of the original legendary Garden of Eden in the majority of the new planetary landmasses.

Now what about the number of human beings who will be able to ascend at this time? The answer is, as many as *wish* to ascend. This may surprise you, but remember that with the new energies which will be coming in, very few will be able to exist at the higher vibrational level – and if you feel uncomfortable at that level, you are not likely to want to opt into the new life. In rather simplified human terms, it will be similar to standing at a doorway on the other side of which there is a world with a steamy jungle atmosphere, or perhaps an icy-cold landscape or even one of blistering heat – certainly conditions which are totally different to those in which you are currently living – and having to make a decision whether to migrate into that world or not.

Whatever choice you make will be irreversible in the immediate future, but you will *realise* that the choice will be yours.

Let us carry out a little experiment, and ask you to calculate what percentage of the population are likely to want to opt into the new life, and let us point out some of its facets.

First, how many of you do you think are prepared to enter a new life where you are totally tolerant of all other human beings, and bear no hatred to, or aversion from anyone at all, regardless of their religion, politics, race, nationality, gender, age, lifestyle or beliefs? How many do you think have reached that stage already?

Next, how many of you are prepared to go without all of the current stimulants which are so part of your modern life, the alcohol, tobacco, drugs, tea, coffee, gambling and entertainment? We can include the stimulant of wanting to outdo others in a business or commercial enterprise, as such things will no longer exist. Are there any of you who are there yet?

After that, how many of you are prepared to live in a society where there is no money, and no impetus to do anything at all for monetary gain? Such experimental societies do exist, although by and large they are still in their infancy.

Now we come onto some of the more difficult issues: how many are prepared to live in a communal society, where there is no need for rivalry with any of your neighbours, no *keeping up with the Jones* mentality, and where there is no concept of being better than anyone else? This would include not only ideas of supremacy on the physical level – seen in your current fascination with spectator sports – but also on the mental, emotional and organisational levels.

Then we have a consideration which would possibly put off a large number of people: how many of you would be prepared to work for the good of the community, playing your part according to your own personal abilities and working hard, without *any* desire for your own personal benefit?

Many of you will ask whether *gender issues* will continue after Ascension, and we have to tell you that they will not. They are issues in human life because of the continuous alternation in successive human lives in masculine and feminine bodies, which are chosen by the soul with the aim of eventual balancing out the polarities of gender. Inevitably – after a period of many hundred lives – there are occasions where someone born in a masculine body after a succession of lives as a woman will have the mind and emotions of a woman, or vice versa. By the time that the soul is ready to ascend all such issues will have been resolved, and each person will have a *choice* of ascending either as a man or as a woman.

Well, putting all those factors together, what percentage of the human beings on the planet do you think are likely to accept a new existence in the *Brave New World* of the next dimension? Do any of you think it is likely to be more than 10%?

For that matter, how did you personally score? Have we put you off the idea of Ascension completely? Of course, the outcome might be slightly different if we outlined some of the benefits of the new existence. For instance, apart from the fact that illness and disease will no longer be a factor, the planet will supply all the needs of its inhabitants – but let us surmise for a moment what those needs might be.

In order to do this, we have to differentiate between what normally happens when an individual ascends and goes into a new dimension, and what could possibly happen on this special occasion. We will consider the former situation first: when an individual ascends, he or she has the choice whether to exist in the new dimension, or to stay connected to the Earth – but in a non-physical body – in order to help those on Earth to make spiritual progress. So let us see what will happen if *you* ascend as an individual and decide to exist fully in the new dimension.

When you read *this* information, you can be *certain* that it is correct, for we have not only been through the process ourselves, but also we have seen it happen to large numbers of other human beings during the long period of time since we ourselves ascended.

In the first place, the new dimension will be one beyond physicality, which means that you will not have a physical body. Now because this would be too much of a shock to your present mental system if you went immediately into the state of being formless, you will for some time have the *illusion* of having a body, and with that will come the *illusion* of having bodily needs. So you will feel the need to eat and drink, and will also look forward to sleeping on a daily basis.

But in fact, rather than being physical, the new dimension will be *mental*, and so you will very soon find *that what you think, is*. If you want to create anything, as soon as you form the idea of what you want in your mind, it will appear – you will not need to go through the laborious processes of bringing it into being, as you have had to do on Earth. Once you have found this out, you will start to experiment with your new abilities, and you might possibly begin with food: just think of your favourite food, however rare or exotic it may be – and there it will be. Change your mind to wanting something else, and once more, it will appear before you.

Of course, at the start there will be a tendency to want to produce and eat food or drink to your heart's content, and this is where you will find another strange fact – that you will never feel over-full, bloated or drunk. You can eat or drink as much as you like, without any appreciable effect. In time, this may well lead you on to experiment further, to see if you can create the effect of being comfortably full, without having eaten at all – and you will find that just the thought of that will create the feeling. So you will eventually realise that you do not really need to eat or drink anything at all – the mere thought of having done so will be sufficient.

Little by little, you will learn that the same is true of every one of the physical needs which you used to have while in a human body. You will get to that state only by experimenting, and the order of your experiments will largely depend on your own history while in an earthly body. One of the interesting things that you will find out is that you have no need of physical sexual contacts in your new life – although that does not mean that you will not have relationships. You will learn how to manipulate the actual fabric of Love itself, and will delight in expressing Love to all whom you meet – the different kinds of love in earthly terms will all be merged into one overall expression. Finally, you will realise that the way of expressing Love in that dimension is immeasurably more fulfilling than the mere physical act of sexual intercourse ever was on Earth.

However, we must mention one facet of your new existence which many of you will perhaps find hard to understand – and even consider as a drawback. You will be living in a world of thought. How can that be a drawback? Well, in your present life you live in a world of thought, emotions, words and deeds – and as you already know – what is said and what is done, by any individual on Earth, may bear little resemblance whatsoever to what is actually felt or thought by him or her. However, in the fifth dimension, what you think is immediately seen by others, as is what you are feeling, so anything less than total honesty is just not possible. You simply cannot say one thing and mean another without it being noticed by those around you. But as having got to that dimension will mean that you have already reached the stage of being totally open, there should not be too much of a problem for you.

So what will you be *doing* in your new environment? Well, this is rather up to you: what would you like to be doing? For a time, most people who have ascended continue to do what they found pleasurable on Earth, but many branch out and do totally different things. Creativity in all its forms is much practised, and many people create new art forms, using material both old and new, and merging the practical with the aesthetic. Music and dance also play a greater part in the lives of many people, and *all* take part and enjoy what has been created, whereas in your present society there are levels of Art appreciation which are largely stratified according to the social class of the individual in the society at large. Also, as there is no sense of rivalry, what is created can be genuinely appreciated without the need for criticism.

Others experiment with colour and shape, and find that the range of colours available in the new dimension are immeasurably greater than those available on Earth. Those who had flower gardens on Earth are particularly delighted to find that they can create previously unknown kinds of plants, or assign new colours to existing favourites – even creating that unattainable royal blue rose, for instance. Many will be amazed to find that black is not merely dull and matt, as in earthly Nature, but can be used as a vibrant glowing colour in flowers.

Some might feel a burning need to do service to others, because they have been in one of the caring or service professions while on Earth – and will find that there are ample opportunities to return to Earth and influence human beings still on Earth. We have already mentioned the possibility available to all human beings of calling on discarnate beings for help, and this is the kind of service that those who have ascended quite often do. It might be service to former friends or relatives from the previous existence, or it might be to total strangers – it does not matter. If the need to serve others is there, it does not matter who those others are. Even if the human beings are of a different race or nationality there is no bar to serving them: all communication is on a mind-to-mind basis, so there are no problems of language. Often, of course, discarnate beings are drawn to someone on Earth with whom they feel a special affinity, either because they have traits of character in common or because on Earth they did the same kind of work as the other person is currently doing.

Many who on Earth have been of a more reflective or contemplative disposition take advantage of the immense libraries in the Halls of Learning, which contain information on every possible subject in the universe, and find to their amazement that there is no need to physically *read* a book in order to find out its contents: it is sufficient to merely *hold* the book and *sense* the contents. Those who wish to attend lectures on any subject which is of interest to them similarly find that as communication is on a mind-to-mind level, mere *attendance* at the lectures is sufficient to understand what is being communicated.

So we have discussed what normally happens when an individual ascends, and has the choice of either existing completely in the new dimension or working with someone – or some others – on Earth. But what about the new situation where the people who are ascending en masse are doing so *at the same time as the planet*?

Well, this is where we are all in totally new territory, as it has never been done before. So all that we can do is to *surmise* what the likely effects will be. However, we point out that for us *surmise* does not mean to make a wild guess at what may possibly happen. It means that we have studied all the relevant known factors and have come to the best estimate of the *probable* outcome.

The first thing that we should say is that when individuals ascend in the normal way, they enter into a totally new dimension – *obviously* new – and have to get used to the conditions in this new dimension. We have said that they are given the illusion of still having physical bodies as a *cushion* to avoid them suffering too much stress, but then they very quickly adjust to the new situation. However, in the situation which is now imminent, not only will there be very large numbers of people ascending at the same time, but they will ascend *with* the planet, which means that, to all intents and purposes, *there will be no difference between their future relationship with the planet and their existing one.*

So those who have ascended will not immediately *know* that they have ascended, and will continue to carry on a normal human existence, but in a totally different environment to any which they have already known. They will, in fact, be in exactly the same situation as those people many centuries ago who colonised new territories or lands: they will be pioneers – very important pioneers, as they will prepare the way for the future colonists of the New World Order. They will have lived through the massive physical changes undergone while the planet has been cleansing herself, and will believe that they are the only ones who have survived physically.

* * *

It is very probable that the new colonists will come together in small groups, as they will feel the need for safety. Not realising their new status, they will not know that they are now *totally* safe wherever they go. They will set up small communities, in which everyone will be seen to have a part to play in the success – they will see it as survival – of the community as a whole. Why do we say small communities? Because the high-level vibrations of the new energies sweeping across the universe, and raising the planet itself into a new dimension, will mean that there are not large numbers of people left together in any one place, even in former towns and cities.

What has happened when other planets in other star-systems across the universe have ascended is that the planets themselves have entered the new dimension, while their inhabitants have either been transported to other – similar – planets to continue their own evolution in their existing dimension, or have chosen to end their existence on the planet, in order to be re-born on the destination planets after conditions have become more stable there. We believe that it is likely to happen in a similar way in your own case – the only difference will be that some of the present inhabitants of Earth will be able to enter the new dimension *with* the Earth, and will have a relatively seamless transition from the current world to the new conditions.

There is another planet which lies within your solar system which is suitable for a mass migration of the majority of inhabitants of your Earth – something which will dumbfound your scientists, who have been looking for earth-like planets in far distant star-systems for many years. The reason that it is undiscovered is that it is not detectable by any Earth-based instruments, as it lies on the *opposite* side of your sun, at a similar distance from it as the Earth. Transportation would not be a problem: some of your more imaginative Science Fiction writers have already explored the possibility of moving people from one place to another without physical vehicles, and they will be pleased to find that such a means of transport is indeed possible. However, that is only a small part of the galactic technology which could be made available – your ancient and modern legends of space-ships are firmly based on actual fact.

We believe that the vast majority of the population on Earth, when faced with the choice of travelling to a new planet in relative safety and comfort or taking their chance of survival by staying on Earth while she goes through her cleansing period would choose the former.

We have said that there will be massive disruption of the Earth's surface during the cleansing period, and at that time large numbers of those who have opted to stay behind will die – in your terms: we prefer to say that they will make their transition to the fourth dimension, as that is what it really is. There is always a certain amount of suffering during natural disasters such as earthquakes, floods, tidal waves or hurricanes, and this will be the same at that time. But strange to relate, at the final moment, there will be no suffering at all for those who are not able to ascend with the planet. There will be a massive wave of conscious energy which will sweep across the Earth, and all who are not compatible with this energy will make their transition, in an instant. An analogy in human terms would be that when you pass a large charge of electricity through a lowly-rated electrical fuse, the energy will blow the fuse – and this is exactly what will happen to all who do not ascend.

But does not this imply a prior separation of those who will ascend and those who will not? Of course it does, but as we have already pointed out it is *you*, each one of you, who will decide on your future destination. In many of your religions and cultures you have prophecies of how the division will take place, and phrases like "the sheep and the goats," "the wheat and the tares," "the just and the unjust" abound. You are told lurid stories of what will happen to those who do not reach the standard, which have had the effect of terrifying countless generations of children – and gullible adults – and ensuring that they followed what they were told that they had to do in order to be saved.

However, the truth is far simpler, and far more reassuring: each of you is going through a process of learning, and once you reach a certain stage you automatically gravitate to the next stage. At school, when you came to the end of your school year, and had reached the appropriate standard, you went up into the next grade. In many school systems, you can not move on until you have passed a certain exam, and if you never pass that exam you stay in the same class until the end of your schooldays. Well, the process of life is in some ways similar: however, sooner or later *everyone* reaches the standard, and moves up to the next class. There are no human beings who are left to languish forever in the lower class without hope of progressing. Even more reassuring, there is no one who is ever condemned to eternal damnation, Hellfire, or whatever your accepted name for it is – regardless of how evil they have been during their current life. What they *are* condemned to do is to repeat their time on Earth through apparently endless lives, until they eventually make the grade and can move on.

We hope that this will be a comfort to those of you who love people dearly – perhaps as a parent, sibling or friend – but realise that they can not possibly reach the spiritual level of ascension in their present lives, and so feel that they themselves would not want to ascend and leave their loved ones behind. We would point out that to ascend yourself and leave others behind would merely be the equivalent of emigrating and leaving a member of the family behind, for some valid reason, with the plan that he or she should follow on when conditions became more convenient. In broad terms, you can eventually control only your *own* evolution: you cannot live anyone else's life or decide when he or she is ready to move on.

So let us return to our main theme: you are in a totally new environment, new colonists in this brave new world, and living in small communities. You are without most of what you consider to be the necessities of life in your present existence, since the massive destruction which has occurred while the Earth was cleansing herself has wiped out all your public utilities, so you are really back to a very basic existence. Those of you who long for a back-to-Nature existence in your present life will certainly have their wishes fulfilled if they ascend. However, you will still have all the knowledge of what your current civilisation's technology has been, as well as knowledge of what former ages achieved without the benefit of modern technology or materials, and this will inspire those of you who are of an inventive frame of mind to create artefacts which will be for the benefit of your new society. In this, of course, you will be greatly helped by your new level of ability to receive inspiration of what to do and how to do it.

Your new community may well contain people of differing races and/or nationalities, differing religions and differing political or philosophical views, but you will realise that you all have to work together for the good of everyone. You will very quickly find out that there are certain rules of conduct that you have to obey – but those rules of conduct will not be handed down to you by any superior authority, civil or religious: they will have to be decided by *you* – all of you, communally. You will at last find out what it is like to live in a *true* democracy, where *everyone* has a say in what is going to take place and can influence the decisions which are taken to affect the group as a whole.

As all of you will have reached a high degree of tolerance for the religious views of others, discussion of those views will lead you to the realisation that all religions have, at the deepest levels, the same basic truths. So in examining – and practising – those basic truths you will arrive at the situation where you will live in total harmony with each other, with the other life-forms on the planet, with the planet itself and with everything else in Creation. As far as political ideologies are concerned, you will rapidly realise that although they might be of value in theoretical discussions about life in complex societies, they have no place whatsoever in ordering relations in the community in which you exist.

You will realise that although all of you have reached the same level of spiritual development, not all of you want to do the same things in your community. So some will be quite content to search for food, others will prefer to grow food, and others prefer to prepare it. Some will like to make things with their hands, others will like to work out better ways of doing simple tasks. Some will be happy to look after children, while others will compose music, and create instruments to play it on. However, the binding factor between all will be the fact that you will *all* work for the good of the whole community. This will be in marked contrast to conditions in your present lives, where the majority of you do things only because you *have* to, not because you *want* to. How many of you are currently living lives where you feel *totally* fulfilled?

In your new life after Ascension, if you have chosen to ascend as a woman you will be able to immerse yourself totally in that role and, what is more, you will find yourself honoured for having chosen it. It will be recognised that those of you who become mothers are providing the greatest service possible to the community, as not only are they securing its survival and growth but also they are ensuring that the community is based on family values. The establishment of strong family units is the ideal base for *any* community – something which many in your modern world seem to have totally forgotten.

Not all women will become mothers, of course, but if not, whatever way you decide to make your contribution to the community you will find no antagonism to you doing it. In time, after many generations, the community will slowly evolve into a matriarchal society, as the centuries of male-domination in your existing world will increasingly become merely a distant memory.

* * *

Relationships between individual members of the community will not be marked by any particular ceremony, but when a man and a woman wish to have a child there will be a special ceremony to celebrate the start of a new family unit, and then another ceremony to welcome the arrival of each new child who is born to them. Women will have a choice of the sex of their child, and birth will be a simple painless process. Once created, the family unit will be indissoluble, and so all children will be brought up in a secure family environment. However, all members of the community will rejoice at the birth of each new child, and looking after children will become an overall communal responsibility. So children will grow up within a family but also within the community, and in this way will soon learn that they are totally wanted, and totally loved – a far cry from the situation of a large number of children in your present world, many of whom are unwanted, unloved and tolerated only so that they can be exploited. Currently, the only situation comparable to what will happen in the new societies is that which exists in cultures which have a tradition of large extended-family units.

As the role of a woman as mother and homemaker will be sacred, and represent the peak of feminine achievement, there will be a return to the traditional skills associated with homemaking, including those of making clothing, spinning, weaving and dyeing. Gradually, over a period of many generations, when the community has evolved into a matriarchal society, the grandmothers will be the most revered people of all.

In fact, it will be realised in time that the greatest repositories of knowledge in any community are the oldest people, as they have had the most experience of life, and so their skill and ability will be increasingly used at all levels to provide teaching in life-skills of all kinds. They will be the story-tellers, and able to tell not only the history of what happened in past times but also *why* things happened as they did – and so will be able to provide a very powerful moral framework to bind the whole community together. This concept of revered elders still exists in many traditional societies on Earth, although with the fragmentation of relationships caused by much of your modern living the value and the wisdom of old people is largely being lost as their status becomes increasingly eroded.

One of the most distressing illnesses of old people in your society is that of dementia. This has always existed, of course, as a side-effect of the natural diminution of the physical faculties with the onset of old age, but it is becoming dramatically more prevalent in your modern times, partially due to the increasing side-lining of many old people from the mainstream of life. However, we have to tell those of you who are old that if you ascend at this time, you will experience a dramatic change in the quality of your life: not only will there not be any physical or mental illnesses from which you will suffer – they simply will not exist – but also your experience and wisdom will be in great demand in the community. So you can certainly look forward to a new lease of life.

Many of you are puzzled by the rapid rise in the number of cases of Alzheimer's in your world, and we have to tell you that there is a simple reason for this. Most of the sufferers are very advanced souls who are highly sensitive, and are more affected by the new energies coming onto the Earth than other humans. They are starting to spend increasingly more time visiting the next dimension, and so progressively withdrawing from daily contact with your world. Although this is causing great distress for their friends and relatives in your world, we have to tell you that they themselves – on a soul level – are not suffering in any way!

The main function of the men will be to produce the food of the community, and this will be done mainly by foraging. Although some small-scale cultivation will exist, there will be little real need for it as the luxuriant vegetation will provide all the needs of the community, and gardening for food production will really be practised more as a pleasant pastime or hobby rather than a serious necessity. The men will be also responsible for building and repairing the dwellings of the community: we hesitate to say houses, as in your present society that word has implications of using the industrial products of mass manufacturing – bricks, cement, steel and the like. In the new dimension the only building materials available will be those which the planet itself produces, stone, clay, wood, leaves and various kinds of fibres and grasses.

You may have noticed that we have not mentioned the subject of hunting, and this is because as a society you will be largely vegetarian. There will be some small-scale raising of animals – goats for milk, sheep for wool and chickens for eggs, and horses will be used for transport, but there will be nothing which compares remotely to your present use of animals and animal products.

One of the natural materials which are normally available is clay, and that will be used by the men to create pottery of all kinds for general household use. In time the products will become more and more decorative, as well as utilitarian, and to achieve this the expert services of women will be called on, as by that time they will have achieved considerable skill in the creation of natural dyes and paints, and their use on all kinds of materials.

Finally, every member of the community will eventually come to the end of their time in that community. So what will happen then, and what will decide when the time has come? Once more, we have to tell you that your time will come when *you* make the decision to move on. Remember that you will have already ascended into the new dimension, although as the planet has done so at the same time you will not at first have realised what your new status is. But as you live through a long life, you will slowly realise that you are no longer bound by the rules of living in a human body, and you will feel the urge to move on, into an independent existence. We say independent, because you will realise in time that there is so much more to do in your new dimension, so much more to learn, that is not connected in any way with the routine of living in a family, even the extended family of a community – and so you will decide to move on.

Let us explain for a moment why we have said that you have lived through a long life: why are we so certain that it *will* be a long life? Once again, in your new dimension there will be no illness, no disease and no karmic lessons to learn; there will be nothing which will cut short a life through accidents, so that the possibility of the sudden and tragic loss of someone before his or her time will no longer exist, and each individual will live a full life into old age.

Now when you feel that it is the end of your time, you will tell everyone and they will accept it without question: after all, it will be *your* decision, and they will realise that they cannot halt your own progression. So there will be a short leaving ceremony, at which you will say your farewells to all the other members, and then you will just disappear from their sight. They will feel no regret, only love for you and happiness that you have finally moved on to a higher existence. Compare that with the dismal scenes on Earth when the comparable parting with your own loved ones occurs. The difference is that the members of the community will all *know* that what has happened is merely another stage in the spiritual progression of another being, and just accept and celebrate it. Of course, an added advantage of the departure in the next dimension is that there will be no physical body to dispose of, so no need for funerary rites.

When it happens to you, of course, you will simply move from the communal life into your independent existence, where you will meet new beings, meet up with those old friends who have already moved on, and will be able to continue to learn more about the function, operation and meaning of the whole of Creation, in the same way as everyone else who ascends as an individual. What a glorious vista!

Some of you will question why we have said that you will all return to what you currently consider a very primitive form of life, when you understand the idea of Ascension as living in a Paradise similar to the original Garden of Eden, having unlimited opportunities to study and learn everything which you want to, and having no need to work in any way at all. This is a very valid question, and indeed that will be the case for each of you if you ascend as an *individual*; but what we have been talking about is what will happen to you if you ascend as a group *at the same time as the planet* – and there is a great difference. Ascending as an individual will mean that you are totally free of ties with Earth, and can go on into the fifth dimension *to do your own thing*: ascending with the planet will mean that you, collectively, take on the responsibility of *creating* the new society which will exist in the *new* Earth.

You all have half-remembered prophecies about the Golden Age which is to come. Did you think it would come on your current planet, which you have almost succeeded in destroying? Did you think as human beings you would be able to clean up the pollution which exists, repair all the damage which has been done, replace the rainforests and save the extinction of the wildlife which your activities have so endangered? Surely there are not many of you who thought that all this was possible? We know that in the classical plays of Ancient Greece, when human beings had got themselves into apparently insoluble problems, the day is finally saved by the appearance of some celestial being, a "deus ex machina" – god out of a machine – who *waves a magic wand* and puts everything right: however, as you will realise if you have followed our outline of the process of Creation, such an event would effectively bypass a large portion of that same process.

We have stated what the most probable scenario is, that those of you who choose to ascend will *create* your own New World, your own Golden Age, by your own efforts, starting from scratch and avoiding all the pitfalls which have led to your planet and your society being in the state where it is at the moment. You will set the foundations of the new society, and in doing so you will fulfil your own destiny, that for which you came into your present incarnation. This is the most wonderful thing of all – that you have already *chosen* to be alive on the planet at this particular time in order to help in the creation of the New World – and in doing so, you will be fully, totally and gloriously fulfilled.

So what will be the date when the Grand Ascension will happen? Well, drawing on the experiences of other worlds, their ascension has come about when the planet, its local star and the Galactic centre of the local galaxy have all been exactly in line, and this has produced the massive surge of energy which has provided the impetus for the process to begin, so we can deduce that the same will occur in your world. That date is the 21st of December, 2012, and curiously enough – or perhaps not so curiously – that is the date on which many of your ancient predictions, from different sources, have focused – so that is the date which at present seems the most likely. But once more, the *exact* timing can only be surmised.

So the final questions which many of you will be asking are "What must I do to get ready for this momentous event? Where should I go so that I can ensure that I will avoid the destructive changes which will take place on Earth? How can I make sure that I have the best chance of ascending?" Well, there is a very simple answer to all of these questions: do nothing, and go nowhere! It is a fact that *you have already chosen* – before you came into this present life – whether or not you are ready to ascend, and you will automatically find yourself in the exact place where you are meant to be. Most of you will choose to continue your existence in another third dimensional world, and will choose to depart before the date of Ascension. If you are *meant* to ascend with the planet, you will *go* with the planet, and your present physical location will mean little or nothing at all. Remember what we have said about the wave of energy which the Earth will experience at that time. Those whose own vibrations are compatible with this energy will ascend, those whose vibrations are not, will not. It is just as simple as that. Two of you could be in the same place, side by side, at the moment of Ascension, and one will ascend and the other not. So there is no point at all in trying to find out the ideal place to give yourself the best chance of survival.

We have given you a simple check list to see how near you are to your own ascension, and using that you can gauge what you could do over the next few years. If you find that you are currently not meeting all of the criteria, what might you be doing to get closer to the optimum state? Can you do anything at all? If you can, do it: if you can't, don't worry about it. Remember that, if it is a fact that you are not able to ascend now, that does not mean that you have permanently missed out. It is not an all-or-nothing situation. Carry on with your life – if you miss this bus there will always be another one. However, perhaps knowing a little about the some of the criteria for eventual ascension may help you to take a good objective look at your life now, and draw your own conclusions.

* * *

21. Summation

And so we come to the end of the channelling process and we leave you with the hope that something that we have said has been of value to you. We do not ask you to believe all that we have said, although from our perspective it *is* true. Much of what we have said is *definitely* true, as we have all experienced the transition from a series of earthly lives to existence in a higher dimension, and then from that dimension to the next one up, where we are at the moment. The predictions which we have made have been based on what we have learnt during our studies into what has happened in other cases, in other worlds, but as we have said, you are currently facing an event which is unprecedented in the history of the universe, so there are no direct parallels which can be drawn to achieve complete accuracy.

As far as the information about the beginning and the evolution of the universe are concerned, that also we have been taught in our present dimension, by those who are far more advanced spiritually than we are, although perhaps the language which we have used has been slightly unfamiliar to your scientists. However, the information about the progression of particles through different degrees of complexity is accurate, as we have witnessed these stages ourselves, and continue to be able to do so. In particular we have been able to witness the evolution of complexity through different life-forms into and through the human body in its present state, and we can assure you that the schema of the physical body interlocking with a hierarchy of subtle bodies, all at different vibrational levels, is correct. This is not, however, an exhaustive treatise on the composition of the human being, but perhaps it will provide a starting point for the future research of some of your medical scientists, and possibly even answer some of the questions which have been puzzling them for so long!

As far as those theologians among you are concerned, perhaps some of the information which you have been given will enable you to step outside the narrow interpretation of your own religious histories into a wider understanding of what the process of Creation has actually been – and of course still is. Perhaps it will enable you to realise that each religion contains the seeds of Absolute Truth, while no religion has the monopoly of that Truth. Perhaps, by an understanding of the scientific basis of Creation itself, it will allow you to understand the inherent nature of the primal Creative Force which you perceive as your own deity. Finally, perhaps, in understanding that there is a continual evolution of the human soul – you may come to realise the illogicality of fundamentalist beliefs which deny the validity of other religions.

We bless you all, in the name of the most fundamental power of Creation, the power of

UNCONDITIONAL LOVE.

Further Reading

Works by several authors have been referred to in the text, and this is a list of those authors and the titles of the books concerned. For a more extensive list of the works of each author please consult the internet.

Hay, Louise

You Can Heal Your Life; Hay House Inc., 1984, ISBN 0-9376-1101-8.

Heal Your Body: The Mental Causes for Physical Illness and the Metaphysical Way to Overcome Them, Hay House Inc., 1984, ISBN 0-9376-1135-2.

Emoto, Masaru

Messages from Water, Vol. 1 (June 1999), Hado Publishing, ISBN 4-9390-9800-1.

Messages from Water, Vol. 2 (November 2001), Sunmark Publishing, ISBN 0-7881-2927-9.

Tomatis, Alfred

Pourquoi Mozart. Essay (French) 1991. Publisher unknown, ISBN 2-8764-5107-7.

Lee Carroll and Jan Tober

Indigo Children – The New Kids Have Arrived. 1998 Hay House Inc., ISBN 1-56170-608-6.

An Indigo Celebration. ISBN 1-5617-0859-3.

Lingerman, Hal

The Healing Energies of Music. 1995. Quest. ISBN: 0-8356-0570-1.

Kiester, Sally and Edwin

The Secret Language of Babies. 2005. Happauge, NY. Barron's Educational Series, ISBN: 0-7641-3249-0.

Acknowledgments

I would like to express my gratitude to four people who have been invaluable in the production of this text.

To Laurene Neeld, an outstanding clairvoyant, who first told me of the beings who were waiting to use me as a channel, and then bullied me incessantly to ensure that the original draft was completed.

To Stephanie ni Mhaille, whose wisdom and advice has guided me spiritually for more than a decade, and who has continually encouraged me.

To Stuart Wilson, who bravely took on the task of reducing my rather meandering prose into something that was considerably more readable.

And finally, to my wife Sybil, whose unfailing patience and good humour have sustained me during the whole process of writing, revising and editing the book.

Ralph Steadman

Index

1st dimensional entities	137	Ladder of possibilities	66
2nd dimensional entities	129	Law of Attraction	21, 54, **119**
Affirmations	134	Law of Change & Stability	24
Angels	149	Life force assimilation	58
Ascension	162	Matter and anti-matter	19, **118**
Astrology	41	Mental body is eternal	57
Auto-suggestion in health	97	Mingling of auras	72
Big Bang	24, **117**	Miracle cures	104
Cause and Effect	16, **49**	Mythical monsters	34
Chakras	59	Numan's journey	50
Changing reality	65	Origins of human Karma	50
Children	84	Particle progression	30
Cosmic energy patterns	109	Past civilisations	138
Cosmic Network	15, **42**	Personal guides	148
Creation v. Evolution	33	Planetary changes	107
Dangers of drug abuse	127	Polarities	117
Dangers of nuclear power	138	Pools of consciousness	30
Diet	60	Possession	139
Different universes	38	Power of attraction – auras	55
Dimensions	38, **124**	Power of thought	57, 62, **65**
Elementals	137	Prayer	100
Entities cause depression	131	Primal energy	19
Feral gangs	48	Primary particles	28
Free Will v. Predestination	56	Producing a human being	40
Global warming	107	Psychic gifts	63
Going with the Flow	115	Psychic protection	73
Grounding	141	Psychic receptors	**58**, 61
Healing	101	Psycho-medical causes	74
Homeopathy	102	Schizophrenia	140
Human experiment	34	Sound and Music	152
Impurities	139	Subtle bodies	35
Infinity	21	Terminal illness	104
Intelligent energy	25	The end of the universe	120
Interconnectedness	20	The Fall – fallen angels	143
Inter-dimensional travel	125	The lightning effect	51
Kali Yuga	48	Theory of Everything	28
Karma	68	Thought and health	98
Karmic reward	87	Tom and Harry	66
Karmic turning point	52	Units of consciousness	29
		Visualisation in healing	99

Where there are several entries for a topic, the main entry is in bold type.

About the Author

After getting a Law degree in 1954, Ralph Steadman spent 9 years in the Army, mostly in Army Education. Returning to civilian life in 1963 he worked for IBM for a time, before having experience in Insurance, Construction and the Road Transport Industry, mostly in management or advisory positions. He ended his working life by doing what he most loved – teaching – and retired in 1999. He now lives in Torquay, Devon with his second wife – a clairvoyant healer – and lists as his interests Music (playing the keyboard), Computers and Spiritual Philosophy.

He says of himself, "For the last 50 years I have been interested in psychic phenomena in general, and spiritual philosophy in particular, but in the last two years spent in writing this book I think that I have learnt more about the subject than I have in all the preceding time!"